MIMESIS
INTERNATIONAL

PHILOSOPHY
n. 33

CW00470333

MAURIZIO FERRARIS AND ENRICO TERRONE

CINEMA
AND ONTOLOGY

MIMESIS

© 2019 – MIMESIS INTERNATIONAL
www.mimesisinternational.com
e-mail: info@mimesisinternational.com

Isbn: 9788869771606
Book series: *Philosophy*, n. 33

© MIM Edizioni Srl
P.I. C.F. 02419370305

TABLE OF CONTENTS

INTRODUCTION

This book is the result of some ten years of joint work. On the ontology side, Maurizio Ferraris has developed a document-based account of social reality and has defended a realist conception of philosophy as a systematic investigation on the real world that living beings share through their perceptual capacities and modify trough their social practices. On the cinema side, Enrico Terrone has explored the place of moving images in a document-based social reality and has highlighted the connections between philosophical realism and cinematic realism. This path of joint research has developed along five theoretical dimensions that correspond to the five chapters of this book, namely, art, realism, technology, mobile phones, and animals.

The first chapter proposes an ontological account of works of arts as special social objects, which belong to the category of automatic sweethearts. Films are paradigmatic instances of the latter category and thus, if art essentially is a production of automatic sweethearts, films are to be considered paradigmatic works of art.

The second chapter analyzes the varieties of realism that are relevant to cinema and the way in which cinematic realism relates to philosophical realism. In particular, the chapter considers the notion of a "new realism" and its role in both the history of cinema (under the label "neorealism") and the history of philosophy (as opposed to postmodernism).

The third chapter explores the technological roots that cinema shares with social reality. The methodological assumption is that technology reveals the essence. The more a social practice undergoes a technological development, the more its ontological structure is made explicit and becomes accessible to philosophical knowledge and reflection. From this perspective, digital technologies constitute a priceless ontological resource that allows us to shed light on the nature of social reality (for instance, by considering how social networks work) as well as on the nature of cinema (for instance, by considering how computer graphics works).

The fourth chapter focuses on a particular technological device that is relevant to both social reality and cinema, namely, the mobile phone. This device gives one the opportunity, whenever one needs or wants, both to create social objects by filling forms or signing contracts and to make films by just recording what is going on in one's immediate surroundings. In this sense the mobile phone is a formidable bridge between cinema and ontology.

The last chapter considers a dimension of both ontology and cinema that we take to be somehow complementary to technology, namely, animality. Anti-realism in philosophy often derives from overestimating the creative power of human thought and language. In this sense, paying attention to what human beings share with other animals, first of all sensory experience and perception, can be an important moment of a realist ontology. We argue that cinema, in virtue of its special relationship to sensory experience and perception, can reveal the animal essence of human beings with an expressive force that is rarely available to other forms of art. On the other hand, cinema, as a technological form of art, helps us to also highlight the crucial role of technology in our lives. Cinema and ontology thus reveal themselves to be connected both by technological and animal links. We live in a world inhabited by technological animals that ontology analyzes through concepts and cinema depicts through sounds and images. This book is about all of this.

ACKNOWLEDGMENTS

The chapters have their origins in papers previously published. Chapter I contains material from Maurizio Ferraris's paper "L'opera d'arte come fidanzata automatica" (2011), *Rivista di estetica* 26 and from Maurizio Ferraris and Enrico Terrone's (2017) "Automatic Sweethearts Without Names: The Place of Films in the World of Art", in *A History of Cinema Without Names/2. Contexts and Practical Applications*, edd. Diego Cavallotti, Simone Dotto, Leonardo Quaresima, Milano-Udine, Mimesis International. Chapter II contains material from Enrico Terrone's (2013) "Dal verismo al vetrismo", Fata Morgana, n° 21 and from Maurizio Ferraris and Enrico Terrone's (2017) "Che c'è di nuovo nel realismo? Filosofia e cinema alla riscoperta della realtà", in G. Carluccio, E. Morreale, M. Pierini (eds.), *Intorno al neorealismo. Voci, contesti, linguaggi e culture dell'italia del dopoguerra*, Milano, Scalpendi. Chapter III contains material from Enrico Terrone's (2009) "La cineteca di Babele. Per una nuova ontologia del film", *Rivista di estetica* 42 and from Enrico Terrone's (2014) "The Digital Secret of the Moving Image", *Estetika: The Central European Journal of Aesthetics*, LI/VII. Chapter IV contains material from Maurizio Ferraris and Enrico Terrone's (2011) "Doppia firma. Ontologia del Mobile Movie", *Bianco e Nero* 568 and from Enrico Terrone's (2012) "Cinema, metacinema, telefonini e stupidità. Una risposta a Umberto Eco" *Segnocinema* 177. Chapter V contains material from Enrico Terrone's "Antropocentrismo e cinema di fantascienza" (2011), *Fata Morgana* 14 and from Maurizio Ferraris's (2015) "Cinema per bambini e animali", *Animot* 4.

Both authors made equal contributions to the project of this book. Maurizio Ferraris directly wrote I.1, V.2, and sections from 1 to 5 of I.2, sections 2, 3, 4 of II.2, sections 2, 4, 6 of IV.1. Enrico Terrone directly wrote II.1, III.1, III.2, IV.2, V.1, and sections from 6 to 12 of I.2, sections 1, 5, 6, 7 of II.2, sections 1, 3, 5 of IV.1.

All the texts, except the introduction and III.2, which were directly written in English, has been translated from Italian to English by Sarah De Sanctis.

ART

1.
THE ARTWORK
AS AN AUTOMATIC SWEETHEART

1. *Introduction*

In this essay I propose some ideas for a definition of the ontology of the work of art. My first move is to reject the prevailing twentieth-century continental ontology of art, which conceived of art as a sort of superior and alternative reality to that of science. The second lies in seeking the lowest common denominator that defines the object of art as opposed to the objects of everyday reality. This is a classic essentialist question, which can be summarized in these terms: what is the difference between a screwdriver and a work of art, be it a painting, a novel or a statue?[1] Under what conditions can a screwdriver become an artwork?

This issue has been widely tackled in the field of analytic aesthetics[2], and I wish to address it by taking cue from Roberto Casati's suggestion[3] that the "work of art" genus is characterized by the fact of acting as a "conversation topic." This indication, in my view, provides a precise definition of the artwork in terms of ordinary objects and ordinary reality (conversation has nothing magical about it), placing the artistic object within everyday reality.

However, in my opinion, Casati's definition describes the identity of the work from the point of view of its creator's intentions. I would therefore like to try to answer the question: what is a work of art for the user? Why does one buy those objects we call artworks, perhaps saving on goods of more evident usefulness? Because we are all sentimental, and artworks – in my hypothesis – are artifacts intended to arouse feelings, just as screwdrivers are artifacts designed to screw or unscrew and pints of beer are intended to provoke a state of pleasant relaxation which, however (as we shall see) constitutes a state of mind rather than a feeling.

---

1   It may be objected that a statue and a book constitute very different objects, at least as much as a statue and a screwdriver, but I will clarify this point after explaining my hypothesis in further detail.

2   Danto 1981, Margolis 1999, Zangwill 2001.

3   Casati 2003.

To capture this aspect, I suggest (for reasons that I will clarify) that we consider the artwork as an "automatic sweetheart", i.e. (1) as a medium-sized physical object, which (2) – contrary to a screwdriver – elicits feelings in the user; feelings that (3) – contrary to beer – are not mere states of mind but presuppose a reference to the external world (in this sense I believe I can solve the question of the "truth of art"); and that however (4) – contrary to a gun held to one's head – are experienced with a peculiar disinterest (the aesthetic disinterest, precisely); and that finally (5) – contrary to what happens with a real sweetheart – do not require an interpersonal recognition, because an automatic sweetheart cannot give anything like that.

2. *Continental Ontology of Art*

The first task, as mentioned, is to disprove the concept of "art" as an object of extraordinary experience, which I propose to define as the Continental Ontology of Art. The standard text for this perspective is Gadamer's *Truth and Method*[4]. In it, following Heidegger's indications – which I will mention in a moment – the author declared that he did not want to propose a philosophy of art (considered as an aesthetic variation to be attributed to the Hegelian thesis about art as a thing of the past), but rather an ontology of art, meaning that art is a source of reality even superior to that of science[5].

The ultimate result of the Continental Ontology of Art is postmodern immaterialism, namely the idea that everything, including the moon and the stars, is socially constructed[6]. This would be enough to put the Continental Ontology of Art in a bad light, but as we shall see, there's more. Its biggest flaw, complementary to its diffused aestheticization (that is, the transformation of the world into a kind of work of art, considered as something dreamy and unreal), is that this ontology does not tell us at all – precisely because of this widespread aestheticization – what a work of art is. Indeed, in its hypothesis, even a colourful plastic lighter can be one – and the same, ultimately, can be said even for a screwdriver, a beer, a gun held to one's head and a real-life sweetheart.

---

4   Gadamer 1960.
5   Obviously, Ingarden (1931) had also dealt with ontology of art, but at a time when there was no true distinction between analytic and continental philosophy, which only came into being with Heidegger's departure from phenomenology.
6   As I have extensively argued in Ferraris 1997, 1998, 2001.

So it is natural to wonder how such a position could have arisen in the first place. I believe that the prototypical Continental Theoretician of Art has reasoned more or less like this. "There is art. There is an art market, there are books that tell stories that have not necessarily happened, etc. Why shouldn't there be a philosophy of art? Moreover, in the past two centuries things have happened that have changed the status of art and philosophy. For example, it has been said that art is the organ of philosophy, or that the world has become a fable or an image, or that truth itself is not the conformity of the proposition to the thing, but 'openness' or creation. Why shouldn't there be an ontology of art? Above all, there is science, which claims to give a complete explanation of reality, reducing philosophy to a thing of the past. Instead of being humiliated by science, why should philosophy not form an allegiance with art, and propose an alternative truth?"

Many must have thought something like that, between the second half of the nineteenth century and the first half of the twentieth. Theorists of the sciences of the spirit, philosophers of existence or scholars of artistic things could thus see themselves granted the dubious title of philosophers. Surely Heidegger must have thought this too, in his mid-thirties text *The Origin of the Work of Art*[7], written a few years after *Being and Time*, an ambitious and unfinished work supporting precisely the thesis of art as an alternative truth to science. That text has long constituted one of the main references in the ontology of art: if you cannot have a philosophical ontology (this is the involuntary result of *Being and Time*), you can play the card of artistic ontology.

3. *Metaphysics of the extraordinary: art as "openness"*

In spite of his descriptive attitude, what Heidegger has in mind – just like his enemy Carnap[8], but relying on art instead of science – is actually a prescriptive metaphysics, that is, a metaphysics that teaches us to correct the wrong assumptions we have about the world. Indeed, he supports a very emphatic version of such a metaphysics, because it is one that aims to compete against physics: the being investigated by philosophical ontology is not the same as that of science and not even that of common sense.

---

7   Heidegger 1935.
8   Carnap 1932.

In the specific sphere of the ontology of art, his basic thesis is roughly the following. 1. There is the world of physics, it is already open (i.e., it limits itself to describing what is there). It's not interesting. 2. There is the world of art (and of religion, of philosophy, of morality and of politics). It's interesting, and it opens up. Physics speaks of atoms, fields and forces; ontology speaks of "opening up perspectives". 3. By "openness" he means that art gives us access to a more profound reality than reality itself. 4. This ontology has to do with interpretation, since simple perception or observation have to do with physics. Taking up the examples made about the automatic sweetheart, Heidegger's idea is that, since the artwork makes us understand what the world is, then the automatic sweetheart makes us understand "properly" or "authentically" what is a screwdriver, a beer, a gun held to one's head or a real sweetheart.

Regardless of the success of such a project in the sphere of general ontology, in *Being and Time*, or in subsequent reflections on the history of metaphysics, the underlying problem is that openness is by no means specific to art. On the contrary, it belongs primarily to science and technology as corrective activities: you thought a cup of coffee was getting cold, instead it was coffee giving heat to the surrounding environment; Aristotle believed that there was a tendency to return to natural places, instead it was gravity; Ptolemy believed that the Sun sets, instead it is the Earth revolving around the Sun; and – as far as technology is concerned – wheels and clubs, computers and post-it notes profoundly transform our experience.

Moreover, while even a small technical discovery (like the post-it note) "opens" up, the theory of art as openness supposes that this function is reserved for "great art". It remains to be seen what "great" art is, and above all, what about bad works of art or – which even more interesting – "meh" works of art? In this sense, we would find ourselves in the paradox that a post-it note and a screwdriver open up, while Hayez's *Kiss* does not open anything, and perhaps the same would go for *The Marriage of the Virgin*, if we were to stop liking it.

4. *Metaphysics of the ordinary: art in the "already open"*

It seems difficult to support such an emphatic and improbable view of art that, moreover, has the drawback of not distinguishing the aesthetic experience from technology or science, resulting flawed in relation to its very purpose. A wiser strategy to define the ontology of the work of art (that is, essentially, to say what kind of thing a work of art is) seems to be that of a descriptive metaphysics. The latter does not define art as an extraordinary experience but – quite the opposite – as the quintessence of ordinary experiences, based on average humanity, on a medium size, on invariances (i.e. on elements that are much more stable than the intimate dynamism of science), and on perception (which in a way is the quintessence of averageness).

It may seem frustrating to treat art as the prototype not of an extraordinary entity, but of the most ordinary of objects, next to screwdrivers, beers and guns. But ultimately there is no reason to be disappointed. When Aristotle defined poetry as more universal than history – since the latter describes the particular and the contingent, while the former grasps the universal and the necessary – he implied this exact mediety, and the theory of art as imitation only reinforces the descriptive nature of an ontology of art. Many centuries later, Proust wrote that the task of the work of art is not to show us wonders, but to serve as a telescope or microscope to capture our life. A potential objection at this point could be that I am telling a well-known story here, but I do not think so, considering that a lot of aesthetics seems to have systematically embraced an alternative message, that of the baroque Cavalier Marino: "è del poeta il fin la meraviglia, e chi non sa stupir vada alla striglia". And what is ironic is that art often manages to surprise, but aesthetics hardly ever does.

5. *Conversation topics*

So what do I mean by ontology of the work of art as a metaphysics of the ordinary? More or less something like this: there are existing entities, placed in space and time: tables, chairs, etc. Then there are non-existing entities, which can be inexistent *de facto* (a mountain of gold), inexistent *de facto* and *de jure* (a round-square), formerly-existing (the Roman empire), or subsistent (numbers and relations, for example). Also – and it seems like a good idea – we could add social objects, which exist in time and not in space (doctorates or years of imprisonment). So, in this list, where do we put works of art? It depends on how we define them and, to do so, it is better to find a lowest common denominator: that without which the work of art ceases to be what it is and becomes something else. As we have seen, to say that the work of art is "the setting-itself-to-work of truth" may seem promising at first – given that, at first sight, works of art appear clearly different from screwdrivers and train tickets – but it is ultimately false. In fact, upon closer inspection, screwdrivers and train tickets "open", too. We need to find other criteria.

Herein lies the interest of the theory of art as a "conversation topic". For this theory, artistic objects do not serve for some kind of "communication" between artist and audience – they do not carry messages. They rather arouse attention (and therefore mustn't have an instrumental value) within a linguistic context in which they act as objects of discussion. As I said, the advantage of this theory lies in the fact that it traces art back to an ordinary mediety: we talk about art just as we talk about the weather.

In my opinion, however, this concept applies essentially to contemporary art, which has developed more than ever its own institutions, museums, and critique and has been conceived as a function of these institutions. In fact, "art" (like, for example, "religion" or "philosophy") is a vague concept, or at least more vague than "triangle" or "polenta", and is therefore much more subject to historical determinations. And the notion of "conversation topic" fits the art of the twentieth century much better than that of other periods[9].

6. *Automatic sweethearts*

However, the greatest difficulty of this theory, in my opinion, is the following: what effect is produced by the artwork in the viewer? In short, what does a novel's reader or the visitor of a gallery expect? To converse? Maybe, if we consider the troublesome characters in museums that explain artworks to others without being asked to do so. But there are also sensitive and absorbed people who do not say a word, and who can even experience aesthetic enjoyment in conditions where they could not speak even if they wanted to: for example, Bergotte, Proust's ideal novelist, realizes he is dying in front of a painting by Vermeer, and passes in front of the painting, in the most perfect silence.

So let's find a more specific concept to capture the relationship we have with works of art as users, which, despite the boom of writing (how many people are aspiring writers?) seems to be the prevalent attitude. William James has posed this problem: "I thought of what I called an 'automatic

---

9   Of course one could say that even in the Neolithic period, when people painted caves, they didn't do so as a ritual or to provide information on hunting – which, however, were the most prevalent functions – but they produced, at least in hindsight, topics of conversation. In this case, we would have further proof of the Hegelian thesis that art is a thing of the past: when art is relegated to the past as a claim to truth, when you go to the doctor instead of the shaman, when you use historiated armor as ornament rather than as a means of defence, that's when art is revealed as a topic of conversation ("I love that armor" etc. etc.).

sweetheart,' meaning a soulless body which should be absolutely indistinguishable from a spiritually animated maiden, laughing, talking, blushing, nursing us, and performing all feminine offices as tactfully and sweetly as if a soul were in her. Would any one regard her as a full equivalent? Certainly not, and why?"[10]. It seems like a thought experiment, yet it is the description of a real fact: for the theory that I am proposing, libraries, newsagents, concert halls and art galleries are full of automatic sweethearts, which we call "works of art"[11].

Therefore, the thesis I intend to defend consists in the claim that, from the spectator's perspective, the work of art is the same as James's automatic sweetheart. Like the latter, artworks are physical objects that arouse feelings and sensations just as people do; unlike people, though, they offer nor claim any sort of reciprocity.

Of course, one could object that a landscape, a painting by Mondrian or a symphony do not look like a person at all. I agree: my theory is not that artworks should look like people in the sense of being anthropomorphic, but that people are usually the greatest source of feelings for us – the same feelings that can be aroused by a landscape or a colour (albeit often in reference to people). I hope this point will be made clearer in what follows, but for now I wish to outline a bit better the fundamental characteristics of the present analogy between the artwork and the automatic sweetheart.

7. Perceptions

My first move will be to note the specifically physical nature of artistic objects. Just as an automatic sweetheart, *works of art are primarily*

---

10   James, 1908.
11   After having exposed this hypothesis at a conference, I was submerged by automatic sweethearts, and I thank all those who gave me insights on this point, especially Anna Li Vigni, who was the most generous in terms of cultural references. In the field of literature and theatre: Landolfi, *La moglie di Gogol* in *Ombre*; Rosso di San Secondo, *Una cosa di carne*; *The Sleeping Beauty*; Cormac McCarthy, *Child of God*; Hoffmann, *Wedekind* (to which one could add Proust contemplating Albertine while she is sleeping). In cinema: Lubitsch, *Die Puppe*; Tarantino, *Kill Bill*; Almodovar, *Talk to Her*. I am truly grateful for these references, but I have to make an observation. Often what we see is a passage from the living to the automaton (a coma, an idiot), rarely the other way around. In reality, according to my theory, even a screwdriver (and of course a bottlerack) can be an automatic sweetheart, that is, pretend to be a person despite having no anthropomorphic traits.

physical objects, despite the hopes of conceptual art and (conversely) of postmodernism, which considered art and reality as complementary fictions. Whether art is the domain of appearance (according to Plato) or the sensible appearance of the idea (according to Hegel), this appearance has to manifest itself to human sight, ears and touch[12].

Elsewhere[13], openly rejecting the reduction of art to language (and ultimately to an impoverished form of concept), I have tried to bring the attention to this very point. A concert doesn't change all that much if you hear it on the radio, but an exhibition in the same circumstance would become a very different thing, namely a *description* (whereas the concert would still be a *performance*); furthermore, such a description would be much poorer than – say – a sports commentary, because the latter at least has a purpose, whereas a description of an exhibition doesn't (what we would hear is only data and evaluations). Language itself, in literature, has a very different value compared to when it is used to provide information.

Further proof of this comes from the fact that, in principle, if telepathy were possible there could be telepathic newspapers and telepathic scientific journals, or even telepathic elections, but there could hardly be telepathic poems or novels. The scarce success of audiobooks, or even novels to be read online, seems to support this intuition: aesthetic fruition, even in linguistic arts, requires certain physical components (paper, font, etc.) that are more than the mere transmission of the message. Of course one could imagine new ways to enjoy artworks, and wonder for example how visual art is experienced on the internet. However, physicality is still central both to the fruition of art (I will never be able to truly enjoy an exhibition on my smartphone) and to the very identity of art (it is one thing if they steal my painting, another if they take a picture of it and leave the original where it is). This is truly a crucial point. Museums do not gather memos of the artists' ideas, and a library cannot be replaced by its catalogue. The very strategies to enforce copyright, aiming at the protection of the *literal* formulation, confirm the link between the physicality and the identity of the artistic object[14], which once more reveals its proximity to ordinary objects.

---

12   In § 13 I will explain why it taste and smell are less apt to receive it.
13   Ferraris 1997 and 2001.
14   Ferraris 2003a.

An obvious objection to the physicality of art was raised by Berkeley[15]: when I see a painting representing Julius Caesar I only see patches of colour, the rest is added by the contemplating spirit. In this regard, I would note that the spirit does add something but it adds what is already in the painting. Indeed, even one who knew nothing about Julius Caesar would recognize that person and not another. If then one chooses to represent a pipe and write that "this is not a pipe", the fact remains that everyone can recognise a pipe (or at least a small wooden brown object, if someone didn't know what a pipe was). Therefore my view is that it is correct not to reduce art to perception, because we have many perceptions that are far from artistic. However, I believe that talking about art without reference to *aisthesis*, as many have done till not long ago, is even worse.

8. *The world of artworks*

I would like to clarify this aspect, namely the specific way in which art is linked to perception. I will do so by providing three criteria that, however, are valid as a necessary but not sufficient condition, and serve, at most, to distinguish a work of art from a pure bundle of sensations, and to describe the general characters of the sphere of the world in which artworks exist[16].

1. *Aisthesis: works of art are closer to perception than to interpretation. They are essentially physical objects.* That art has to do with aisthesis is not an opinion, but a fact. Try to replace a concert with the description of the concert, an exhibition with a description of the exhibition, a novel with its summary, or a poem with its paraphrase – you will realize that it is true, as is both intuitively obvious and shown by neurophysiological evidence[17]. This is the reason for Baumgarten's appeal to sensible knowledge, that is, clear but not distinct knowledge, which was already at the center of Leibniz's criticism of the Cartesian identification between clarity and distinction[18]. In this case, this consideration tells us that there is a strong difference between scientific experience and sensible experience, between what we know and what we see (and the interesting aspect is that science clearly supports this difference, which I think differentiates my position

---

15   Berkeley 1713, first dialogue, 226 ff.
16   Developed in Ferraris 2002.
17   Zeki 1999.
18   Leibniz 1684.

compared to romantic revolts against science). Art is primarily connected to the structures of common sense and to naive physics (think of metaphors such as "the sun goes down", etc.)[19]. And, also from this point of view, art is not the discovery of an alternative world to that physics, but a description of the world of experience as it appears outside of physical theories.

2. *Mesoscopy: art has a mesoscopic size.* The world is full of medium-sized things, neither too big nor too small, that is, adequate to our bodily extension and to our ecological resources and needs. I suggest calling this hypothesis "hypothesis of mesoscopy"[20]. Mesoscopy is typical of ordinary experience and therefore (according to my thesis) of the aesthetic experience: artworks are physical objects of a specific size, neither too big nor too small. The problems encountered by Wagner, and even more so by Satie's *Vexations* (24 hours of piano) or by Warhol's *Empire* (a 8 hour shooting of the Empire State Building), confirm this intuition: oversized works are already difficult to enjoy, so imagine how problematic it would be for a symphony that lasted a whole millennium[21]. Kant's sublime designates all that is somehow too large to be represented (according to his thesis that the phenomenon should be medium-sized). The unity of time, place and action in Aristotle also seems to refer to this mesoscopic size. And the psychology of novels also shares the mesoscopic hypothesis: narrative likelyhood, the possibility of sharing feelings or participating in actions, falls within this dimension. I am not saying that the stories told in novels are "mediocre" (if so, they would not be interesting). On the contrary, I am saying that Greek tragedies are medium-sized too, as they talk about mothers who kill children or children who lay with mothers, that is, strong or extreme things, but within our reach: there is nothing in Greek tragedies that does not have an equivalent in the news.

---

19   Consider Shakespeare's *The Taming of the Shrew*: "Thrice noble lord, let me entreat of you To pardon me yet for a night or two; Or, if not so, until the sun be set." "Or if not so, until the Sun has completes its rotation around its axis" doesn't sound as well, and not just for metric reasons.
20   Gibson 1979.
21   Surely it would not be classified as a work of art, if only because no one could hear it entirely. Not to mention the fact that in a thousand years artistic taste would certainly change, and in ten thousand years the very concept of "art" could disappear.

3. *Invariance and unamendability: works of art have a duration in time and a specific consistency, which cannot be changed*[22]. Strawson considered invariance to be the very basis of "descriptive metaphysics"[23]. The basic idea is that while in the periphery of thought, which concerns our most sophisticated acquisitions, things change (or can change) very quickly, there is an invariant core of human thought that does not change (or changes little: this is why we can still respond emotionally to Homer, but we would not adopt the scientific theories of his time). Now, this core certainly includes art, which has typically developed the (immutable or almost so) concept of "classical". Compared to Strawson, I would add that things do not change because they cannot be corrected, *just like perceptions*. Unamendability[24] is the common feature to *aisthesis* and art: if the sheet is white, I cannot see it black, not even by turning off the light (in that case I would not see a black sheet, I simply would not see anything); Sherlock Holmes will live forever in Baker Street, we cannot create an alternative theory in this regard; and Uriah Heep is bad no matter how much we review our notions of morality.

9. *Cosmology and ecology*

To illustrate the three criteria mentioned above, let's take the example of the *Divine Comedy*, which deals with supernatural things and cosmic dimensions – seemingly the opposite of human comedy, which deals with middle-sized things and events. Yet, in spite of the subject matter, I will show that this work's horizon is still that of sensibility, mesoscopy and unamendability.

In fact, the world of Dante is not the *infinite* one of science, which would have revealed itself several centuries later as the cosmos where humanity stands at the edges and the mesoscopic sphere in which we live is intermediate and transitory with respect to the macroscopic and the microscopic ones. However, Dante's world is not even a *virtual* cosmos produced by the paradoxes of a metaphysics that has decided to break with the constraints of the world of everyday experience, like Reverend Edwin

---

22 Thomasson 1999 notes that literature has a temporally greater extent than other arts. A picture cannot be handed down orally as has happened, for centuries, with the Homeric poems; but this does not change the unamendability factor: the very transmission aims at keeping the work unchanged.

23 Strawson 1959.

24 Ferraris 2002.

Abbott Abbott's Flatland (a world with only two dimensions). Dante's world is three-dimensional just like ours. His universe is *ecological*: as Husserl would note in the twentieth century[25], in such a universe the Earth is flat and does not move, and the planet is the ark originating all our meanings and giving sense to the words and metaphors of ordinary language.

The point is relevant. Like Dante, and despite knowing that the Earth is round, Husserl recognizes a perspective in which it is flat. This is the perspective of ordinary life, in which there are no conferences debating who is upside down, whether we or the New Zealanders, because from an astronomical point of view the question is irrelevant, and from an ecological point of view, relevant to the environment in which we live, both us and New Zealanders behave as if we were on a flat land and not upside down at all. Now, this ecological datum also concerns literature, because our feelings and emotions are related to this dimension rather than to the microscopic or macroscopic one. The only possible literary effect of the micro and the macro is the sublime, Pascal's and Leopardi's sense of bewilderment in the face of infinity, and it does not come from the discovery that the earth is round, but from knowing that ours is a world among other worlds, in an endless cold darkness.

This is what I wish to underline, and it holds not only for Dante (who describes the supernatural), but more so for Homer and Joyce, and probably for every literary work: it is difficult to conceive a novel about neutrons (unless they were humanized like Disney's animals), just as it's hard to be moved by *Flatland*, where women are lines, the bourgeois are triangles and the aristocrats pentagons. The entire world of Dante, who was a theoretician of allegory but attentive to literal meanings, is composed of sensible qualities, the only ones that can really move us and convince us by interacting with our ordinary psychology (and is it not the same with the flavour of a madeleine?). Only in this ecological world, where even in the afterlife we do not forget the taste of things, can there be something like Cacciaguida's prophecy: "Tu proverai sì come sa di sale/ lo pane altrui"[26]. Because the bread of others really does taste like salt, even if the one who says so is a kind of ghost. The *Comedy* is set on the same ark-Earth that still bears upon *Star Wars* or *2001: A Space Odyssey*.

---

25   Husserl 1934.
26   *Paradiso*, XVII, 58-59: "Thou shalt find out how salt another's bread/ is wont to taste"

10. *Feelings*

As I said before, referring to perception, to a certain size and to unamendability is a necessary but not sufficient criterion. After all, the world is indeed full of moderate-sized specimens of dry goods[27], which are not works of art. And Andy Warhol's attempt to turn a moderate-sized specimen of dry goods (a Brillo box) into an artwork, just like Duchamp's bottlerack and urinal, are certainly exceptions – which however confirm the medium-size of artistic objects. It seems rather obvious, though, that like all social objects, works of art are objects of a higher order, objects that rely on other objects.

So, having defined the genus, let's define what is specific about artworks. The proposal by which works of art are conversation topics, as I recalled at the beginning, applies to the (mainly, contemporary) production of works of art, but – as I said – it seems to me that it does not explain what users look for in those works. Quite banally, if one can very well write or paint so that people will talk about his writings and paintings, it is much more difficult for one to read or look at a picture with the goal of discussing it with someone else. It is true that, as Kant noted, when I appreciate an artwork I imagine that there is someone in the world who would share my pleasure; but it doesn't mean that in that moment I am hoping to acquire a conversation topic.

Take a lonely teenager reading Salgari or a lifer reading *The Count of Monte Cristo*. Are they doing it for the sake of conversation? Not necessarily[28]: what seems to prevail is the need to kill time and use the imagination. On the contrary, it could be argued that there are types of art objects, such as horror movies and novels, that are best enjoyed alone. Bram Stoker's *Dracula* can be appreciated the most if we read it on our own, at night; if we do so in the daytime surrounded by people it will not quite be the same. Not to mention the spoiling critics who reveal the ending of thriller movies, killing the suspense.

So what is the difference between artworks and other objects? What is it we seek in works of art but not in screwdrivers, beer glasses, vats, honorific titles or PhDs? As I suggested earlier, we essentially seek *feelings*[29]. Hence my second thesis: *artworks are objects that arouse feelings –*

---

27   Austin 1962.
28   A cloistered nun under the vow of silence or a stylite can easily be bearers of artistic experiences.
29   One can be proud of being, say, a knight, but the feeling he has is essentially linked to social recognition. A knight in a jail would be hardly proud of his title.

that is, in accordance with Kant, objects that are related to pleasure and displeasure (and possibly boredom). This thesis may understandably sound unconvincing, as it recalls Croce's theory of art – as well as the latter's problems and inconsistencies. The question, in short, is thorny and I would like to articulate it better.

11. *Croce*

Let's consider the problems with Croce's theory. In fact, it seems easy to say what an artwork is, and it seemed even easier to Croce: it is the union of intuition and expression. If an artwork is such, it will be an honest expression of feeling; otherwise it will be a cold and forced allegory. The same goes for feelings: if the feeling is artistic, it will be warm and true; otherwise, either the artwork is devoid of feeling or it is the manifestation of non-aesthetic elements, perhaps of decadent sensuality. All well and good. But what happens when the philosopher is not just talking to himself about his taste, but to others who may not share it?

The best rejection of Crocian aesthetics (and of the many other kinds that depend on it) lies in cases that are not so obvious: for instance, the 1928 USA vs. Constantin Brancusi trial. The issue at stake was precisely to establish whether the objects Brancusi was taking into the States were or were not artworks – in the former case they would have enjoyed certain tax exemptions. The trial went on for some time[30], and eventually Brancusi won thanks to the judge's self-proclaimed incompetence in the matter, but the point remains that the identity of intuition and expression was of no use to anyone.

It is probably because of cases like this that the sentimental side of art has been completely disregarded lately. The same mistake had been made by idealists: thinking that arousing feelings was not enough, they claimed that art has a special relationship with truth. Now, what I am doing here is not claim that art is primarily sentimental, exposing myself both to the anti-Crocian objection (how can you define a genus based on its effect, especially if the latter is so variable?) and to the idealist one (feelings are not the essence of art, what counts is the truth). I believe things can be made clearer by using one objection against the other.

---

30   And its records are enlightening for anyone who deals with ontology of art, cf. Paleologue-Rowell 2003.

12. *Art and truth*

First of all, I would like to point out that the appeal to sentiments does not help as such to understand what a work of art is, but to solve a *vexata quaestio*, that of the truth of art. My thesis is that the feelings aroused by art, or by the automatic sweetheart, are not fake: the fear I feel when Norman Bates (aka Anthony Perkins), in *Psycho*, turns around on the chair is the same that I would have in reality, it only lasts less and has fewer consequences. And – going from effects to descriptions – it is quite legitimate to use art as the best repertoire for the analysis of feelings. The problem, therefore, does not concern the *truth* of the feelings aroused by an artwork or an automaton, but the *variety* of feelings in question.

Here it is important to consider one thing: *all feelings are true*. If I'm afraid, even if I fear something that does not exist, I'm still *really* scared. The are four points to consider in this regard, on an ascending scale that goes from perceptions to feelings.

1. First, my right arm hurts even if it is a phantom limb: the pain is there, the arm is not, but the words I use are perfectly adequate (and they would be less so if I said "*I believe that* my right arm hurts ").

2. Secondly, I'm really scared even if what scares me is just a hallucination (which is still something: as Austin said[31], if my aunt says she has seen a ghost, she must have seen something).

3. Third, I really feel anxious even if (as in the case of pathological anxiety) there is no object that causes my anxiety; likewise, by definition I can be depressed without there being anything in the external world that causes my depression.

4. Fourth: when I laugh at a novel by Mordecai Richler, I cry for a soppy film, or I am moved by the death of Andrei Bolkonsky or Lucien de Rubenpré, my feelings are absolutely true (the case of comedy is particularly impressive: the best laughs come with jokes, which are fully part of the sphere of works of art, also because – like myth – they satisfy the requirements of "conversation topic" as best as possible).

13. *Fictional objects*

The defining rule of the work of art thus seems to be: X, in the external world, arouses feelings in Y (subject). Pleasure and displeasure are always

---

31   Austin 1962.

pleasure or displeasure of something, and all in all seem to play a more important role than the function of art as a conversation topic.

This appeal to the role of feelings, in my view, might come in handy also in relation to the debates, today very heated, on fictional entities. For example: Madame Bovary is different from a real woman, but she is certainly something, because when we refer to her we refer neither to the Eiffel Tower nor to Count Mosca. What kind of thing is she? One might say that she is a social object (not an ideal object, because unlike a triangle Madame Bovary has a beginning in time). Yet, it seems to me that Madame Bovary is different from the Italian Constitution or a 5 euro banknote[32].

I believe that her defining trait is the fact that she is a social object that arouses feelings, intrinsically and disinterestedly, contrary to the Constitution or a banknote. Here is the most important thing: Madame Bovary, like the automatic sweetheart, arouses *true* but *disinterested* feelings. Let's have a closer look at this aspect, which is crucial.

14. *Aesthetic disinterest*

There are many explanations (religious, anthropological, psychoanalytical) of why we eat lamb at Easter, and then in church we eat the host as the body of Christ. I would like to add another one, which serves to illustrate not the Christian religion, but the special character of aesthetic pleasure. The latter is a singular kind of pleasure because, as Kant (and many after him) explained, it is disinterested.

So what kind of pleasure is it? The theoretical issue of disinterestedness is relevant. From an ethical standpoint, if acting morally means acting disinterestedly, then is it right to help one's friends? And from an aesthetic standpoint, how can we enjoy something that, essentially, demands not to be enjoyed? Herein lies the solution: the taste implied in the aesthetic experience is not the same at play when we eat. *Carmina non dant panem*, indeed. Conversely, eating something is always the sign of interest.

If you think about it, the whole *Critique of Judgment*, which argues for the axiom of disinterested pleasure, is filled with references to food as

---

32 In this sense, Searle's theory of fictional objects seems to face a specular and antithetical difficulty compared to that of postmodernism. For the latter something like the Constitution also counts as a fiction, and for Searle a novel – if one doesn't not want to consider it completely false – is ultimately something that has the same status as the Constitution. For a discussion of this point cf. Johansson 2004.

counterexamples. The Iroquois sachem that about Paris only appreciates taverns and greasy spoons is the emblem of it: he is a barbarian incapable of disinterested pleasure, because he only likes what he can eat. And this is not the only example. Take garden art, which at Kant's time was one of the fine arts. Now, flowers have colour and smell, and Kant concludes that the aesthetic aspect (of both the flower and the garden) lies in the form, not in the matter. Why? To refer once again to the sachem, because matter can be eaten (suppose there are fruit trees in the garden, and consider you can make rose salads). Form, instead, cannot be eaten and therefore it is a disinterested aesthetic pleasure.

Consider another case: the sublime, which for Kant is an excessive form of beauty, either by size (something huge) or by power (an earthquake, a seastorm). Now, once again pleasure for an earthquake or a seastorm (Kant calls it "dynamic sublime" because it shows power, whereas the mathematical one shows greatness) can be felt only as spectators, not actors. Why? Of course because in the latter case we would be interested in not being *swallowed* by the storm.

One last example. For Kant and many others, the highest form of beauty is the human body – once again, if you think about it, the reason is remotely nutritional and closely anthropocentric. Man and women are (normally) not food. A pig, instead, is, which is why there are few paintings (let alone sculptures) representing swines. The film *Babe* makes the pig an aesthetic (and not alimentary) object because it humanizes it, and still lives, representing fruit and sometimes fish or meat, are considered less important than portraits. But in any case they cannot be eaten – at most, they can torture a hungry person.

So here is the moral of the story. The Eucharist, the identification between Christ and the lamb, or between Christ and the fish in early Christianity, would seem to be a move against aestheticization. The sacrifice remembered at Mass is not a representation (object of disinterested pleasure), it is not a tragedy with possible cathartic effects, but should arouse real interest, an identification. How? By eating the host. Counter-proof: imagine a mass in which the host was simply shown, and no one, not even the officiant, would eat it. It would be at best a sacred representation, a kind of theatre, a historical or allegorical re-enactment, but it would not be real.

15. *States of mind*

Now that we have exhausted (or almost) the question of feelings, one may ask: do we need an object to arouse feelings? Many would be tempted to answer negatively. Sometimes, it seems, a memory is enough to produce a feeling, as a consequence of which the whole theory of art as aisthesis that provokes feelings would disappear. But I would like to point out that any memory is a memory of *something*.

This brings me to a third point, perhaps a little less obvious, even if it is simply the other side of the previous one: *all feelings (including anxiety) require an external world*. It does not make much sense to ask oneself if one is truly happy, or if one only believes to be so; instead, it makes sense to ask ourselves if there really are, outside our mind, the things that make us happy. This is part of the definition of feeling: we are happy or unhappy for something or for someone, otherwise we would suffer from euphoria or depression, which are not exactly feelings, but states of mind that do not have a cause in the outside world[33]. Antidepressants warn about the fact that they can provoke euphoria: they never say they could cause happiness; in the same way, it seems difficult to consider the intake of a hallucinogen as an artistic experience.

In fact, feelings are different things. We say "what are you laughing (or, more rarely, crying) about?" when we do not see the thing that causes the reaction, because there must be one. Hence the strangeness of anxiety, which has no reference in the external world, yet has the aspect of a feeling (Heidegger rightly said that its object is nothingness). For example, it is difficult to conceive of a feeling such as jealousy or shame in an absolutely solipsistic structure (and when Sartre observes that even a solipsist is ashamed if he is caught spying through the keyhole it simply means that it is rare to find hardcore solipsists, and if there were any they would not be ashamed).

This point is relevant. For example, can one say that an absolutely autistic subject has feelings in the same sense in which we have them? Does he love his mother in the normal sense of the word "love"? Most likely not. Likewise, and essentially for the same reasons, an absolutely autistic subject[34] would hardly (or never, by principle, according to my theory) have an aesthetic experience, because the latter by definition presumes a reference to an object in the external world.

---

33   Magri, ed. by, 1999.
34   Bloom 2004, pp. 23 ff.

16. *Acknowledgment*

So far, so good: the artwork is like a person, and seems to want to say something, but this is where the analogy ends. Hence the fourth point, which allows me to provide the key criterion to define the work of art: *some feelings require acknowledgment from other people*[35], something that neither art nor an automatic sweetheart can give. The works have no conscience, nor do they have sensitivity, just like machines and, among these, automatic sweethearts: "'One day', said Wilcox, 'there will be lightless factories full of machines like that.' 'Why lightless?' 'Machines don't need light. Machines are blind'"[36], And this makes a huge difference.

Think about friendship. Do I use the word "friendship" correctly when I call myself a friend of someone who does not know me? It would seem not, as Aristotle had already noted emphasizing the intimately social and political character of friendship[37] (whereas I can very well hate someone who does not know me and whom I envy). The same applies to "politeness"[38]: if by hypothesis one was the only man on the face of the Earth, he could hardly be said to be "polite"; in the same way, it would be bizarre and inappropriate to claim that a solitary person has good taste, while it is not hard to imagine her being scared or bored.

For me to feel friendship, politeness, and taste, not only must there be an outside world, and I must not be an automaton, but it is also necessary that the other person knows me. Which is exactly what the automatic girlfriend – and therefore art – cannot do. The moral of the story, after all, is very simple: to say that a book may be a friend, however nice it may sound, is wrong. If there is one thing that the work of art cannot do, it is being friends, even if it does many of the things that are usually attributed to friends: keep us company, help us in difficult times, entertain us, make us gossip. Like an automatic sweetheart, *works of art are objects that pretend to be subjects*. This fiction – the only one – is decisive, both because it allows us to differentiate the beauty of art from the beauty of nature, and because it distinguishes the work of art from other types of artifacts, such as screwdrivers or vats, which do not pretend to be subjects endowed with intentions (until they are exhibited in a museum, with a title and a signature).

---

35 See Bloom 2004, also on this point.
36 Lodge 1989, p. 85.
37 Derrida 1994.
38 Perconti 2003.

17. *Conclusion*

I'll conclude by summarizing the essential theses that I have presented to indicate what kind of object (ordinary and not extraordinary) a work of art is.

1. Works of art are primarily *physical objects* of a given size, neither too large nor too small, neither too extensive in time nor too instantaneous.
2. Artworks are objects that provoke *feelings*, which are true (I do not pretend to cry when watching a sad film) but *disinterested*, since I am a spectator and not an actor.
3. Feelings arise precisely because the works are experienced as things in the *external world*. They therefore differ from, for example, hallucinogens, which cause certain states of mind that are only internal.
4. Artworks, however, unlike people, cannot reciprocate our feelings. They *do not acknowledge* them. And after all they are right to do so, since those feelings may be true but they are really too disinterested.

Now, the artwork and the automatic sweetheart pass the same test, because the automatic sweetheart is also a physical object placed in the external world that arouses disinterested feelings but is not able to recognize us. A screwdriver, a beer, a gun held at one's head and a real girlfriend in normal health conditions, however, do not pass this test. This is what I wanted to prove, and this is where I'll conclude this essay.

Bibliographical References

Austin, J. L. *Sense and sensibilia,* Oxford, Oxford University Press, 1962.

Berkeley, G., *Three Dialogues between Hylas and Philonous* (1713), Oxford, Oxford University Press, 1998.

Bloom, P. *Descartes' baby: how the science of child development explains what makes us human*, New York, Basic Books, 2004.

Carnap, R., "The Elimination of. Metaphysics Through. Logical Analysis of. Language" (1932), in A. J. Ayer, ed., *Logical Positivism*, Glencoe, Illinois: The Free Press, 1959, pp. 60-81.

Casati, R. "The unity of the kind 'Artwork'", *Rivista di estetica*, n.s., n. 23, 2003, pp. 3-31.

Danto, A. C., *The Transfiguration of the Commonplace. A Philosophy of Art*, Cambridge, Mass., Cambridge University Press 1981.

Derrida, J., *Politiche dell'amicizia* (1994), tr. it. di G. Chiurazzi, Milano, Cortina 1995.

Ferraris, M., *Estetica razionale*, Milano, Cortina 1997.

Ferraris, M., *L'ermeneutica*, Roma-Bari, Laterza 1998.

Ferraris, M., *Experimentelle Ästhetik*, Wien, Turia und Kant 2001.

Ferraris, M., "Inemendabilità, ontologia, realtà sociale", in *Rivista di Estetica*, ns., 19, 2002, pp. 160-199.

Ferraris, M., "Problemi di ontologia applicata: la proprietà delle idee", in A. Bottani e C. Bianchi, a c. di, *Significato e ontologia*, Milano, Angeli 2003, pp. 104-115 (=Ferraris 2003a).

Ferraris, M., "Perché gli estetici non possono non dirsi crociani", proceedings of the conference "Croce in Piemonte", University of Turin, May 2003 (=Ferraris 2003b).

Gadamer, H. G., *Truth and Method* (1960), London, Bloomsbury Academic 2004.

Gibson, J.J., *The Ecological Approach to Visual Perception*, Boston, Houghton Mifflin 1979.

Heidegger, M., *The Origin of the Work of Art* (1935-36), in *Off the Beaten track*, Cambridge, Cambridge University Press 1950, pp. 1-50

Husserl, E., *Reversal of the Copernican Doctrine in the Interpretation of the Current Worldview,* (1934), in Marvin Farber & Edmund Husserl (eds.), *Philosophical Essays in Memory of Edmund Husserl*, Cambridge: Mass., Published for the University of Buffalo by the Harvard University Press 1940

Ingarden, R., *The Cognition of the Literary Work of Art* (1931), Evanston, Illinois, Northwestern University Press, 1973.

James, W. "The Pragmatist Account of Truth and Its Misunderstanders", *The Philosophical Review* XVII January 1908 (reprinted in The Meaning of Truth).

Johansson, I., "John Searle and Barry Smith on Money and Fictional Objects", paper presented at Ifomis, University of Lipsia, June 2004.

Leibniz, G. W., *Meditations on Knowledge, Truth, and Ideas* (1684), *Leibniz: Philosophical Essays*, Cambridge, Hackett Publishing 2015, pp.23-38

Lodge, D., *Nice Work!*, London, Secker and Warburg, 1988.

Magri, T., a c. di, *Filosofia ed emozioni*, Milano, Feltrinelli 1999.

Margolis, J., *What, after All, Is a Work of Art?* Penn State University Press 1999.

Meinong, A., *The Theory of Objects* (1904) *Realism and the Background of Phenomenology*, Illinois, Free Press 1960.

Nussbaum, M. C., *Love's Knowledge*, Oxford, Oxford University Press 1992.

Paleologue, A. – Rowell, M., *Brancusi contre États-Unis. Un procès historique, 1928,* Paris, Adam Biro 2003.

Perconti, P., *La mente tra le teste. Interpretazionismo radicale*, relazione al Convegno Sifa 2003.

Putnam, H., *The Threefold Cord: Mind, Body and World*, New. York, Columbia University Press, 1999.

Schaeffer, J.-M., *Adieu à l'esthétique*, Paris, Presses Universitaires de France 2000.

Strawson, P. F., *Individuals: An Essay in Descriptive Metaphysics,* London, Methuen 1959

Thomasson, A. (1999), *Fiction and Metaphysics*, Cambridge Studies in Philosophy

Zangwill, N. *The Metaphysics of Beauty*. Cornell University Press, 2001.

Zeki, S., *Inner Vision: An Exploration of Art and the Brain*, Oxford, Oxford University Press 1999.

2.
AUTOMATIC SWEETHEARTS
WITHOUT NAMES
The Place of Films in the World of Art

1. In a 1908 article entitled "The Pragmatist Account of Truth and Its Misunderstanders", William James proposed the following thought experiment:

> I thought of what I called an 'automatic sweetheart,' meaning a soulless body which should be absolutely indistinguishable from a spiritually animated maiden [...] Would any one regard her as a full equivalent? Certainly not, and why? Because, framed as we are, our egoism craves above all things inward sympathy and recognition, love and admiration. The outward treatment is valued mainly as an expression, as a manifestation of the accompanying consciousness believed in.

The experiment shows that when interacting with someone we are not satisfied with one looking like a person: we want one to really be a person. However, there is a category of objects with which we normally interact being content with the fact that they resemble people, though clearly not being such. These objects are works of art.

The theory of the work of art as an automatic sweetheart (see Ferraris, 2007, and the previous essay in this book) aims to treat the work of art as a social object while preserving its aesthetic peculiarities. These two complementary objectives are pursued through the articulation of two concepts: first, we define a social object as a social act (i.e. involving at least two agents) that is inscribed (i.e. recorded on a tangible medium, or simply in people's minds); second, we define a work of art as a social object that has a peculiar property – being an automatic sweetheart, that is, *an object pretending to be a subject, a thing pretending to be a person.* The (at least two) people involved in the social act, in this case, are the artist and the appreciator. The structure of the automatic sweetheart clarifies the relationship between these two agents: the artist creates the automatic sweetheart as if it were a person and the appreciator experiences it as if it were a person.

2. The obvious objection that a film or a symphony don't look at all like a person allows us to make a decisive clarification. The theory does not state that works of art should look like people in the sense of being anthropomorphic. The idea is rather that usually people are the main sources of mental attitudes – such as emotions and feelings – that are also aroused by works of art.

Also, a work of art pretends to be a person in the sense that it appears to be equipped with its own individuality; the work is presented as an individual to which we are inclined to attribute not only material properties (small, coloured...) but also mental ones (intelligent, brilliant, melancholic, passionate). According to Peter F. Strawson (1959), people are the paradigmatic case of entities that we can describe using both predicates designating material properties (M-predicates) and predicates designating personal or mental properties (P-predicates). Arthur C. Danto (1981, 104) shows that a similar duality of predicates is also found in the case of works of art:

> The relationship between the work and its material substrate is as intricate as that between mind and body. Or, following P. F. Strawson, with his distinction between P-predicates and M-predicates, it is as if there were properties of the work exemplifying what we may call W-predicates and properties of the mere things that are visually indiscernible from the work, exemplifying what we may call O-predicates, where there is the task, which may vary from item to item in an arrayed example, of determining which O-predicates are also W-predicates and which are not. [...] The distinction between artworks and mere real things reappears as a distinction between the language used to describe works and the language of mere things.

We argue that to appreciate a work of art means to interact with an individual that could be called a quasi-person, or an automatic sweetheart: though it has only material properties, it appears to us as if it also had mental properties. Moreover, like people, works of art often have a name (their title) and a date of birth (the time of their creation). Strawson himself, in his only essay on aesthetics (1966), highlights the unique "individuality of the work of art", which distinguishes it from other families of objects. To this end, Strawson endorses the claims of two "writers on aesthetics": Stuart Hampshire, for whom "'[The] purpose [of the critic] is to lead people to look at precisely this unique object, not to see the object as one of a kind, but as individual and unrepeatable"; and Margaret Macdonald, for whom

"Every work of art is unique and in the last resort, perhaps, can be judged by no standard but its own" (quoted in Strawson, 1966, 201).

3. However, some art appreciators are not satisfied with the works of art being *like* people; they want them to really *be* people. To achieve this aim, the work of art must be provided with extra soul, which is the soul of its author. In so doing, not only does the work of art seem like a person, but it *is* a person, in the sense that it becomes inseparable from the author who created it, from whom the work thus receives a supplement of soul.

The cult of the author in the appreciation of art (for instance, the so-called *politique des auteurs* in cinema), seems to respond precisely to this dissatisfaction with the artwork being *like* a person – it is required to *be* a person instead. However, this attitude towards art is likely to have a misleading effect on aesthetic appreciation. The problem is that, according to cult of the author, the value attributed to a work no longer depends on what makes it such – its ability to be like a person – and is instead made to depend on its being a person, that is, its being at one with the author who created it.

In fact, the principle that anything can be a work of art – one of the fundamental principles of contemporary art, ever since Duchamp – has as its indispensable corollary the intentional act of an author who gives the ordinary object an extra soul. A more prosaic way of formulating this fundamental principle lies in the injunction: "read the catalog". If the work does not speak to you, it's not its fault (it is not that it fails to be like a person, to function as an automatic sweetheart): the fault is yours because you do not understand (you, the viewer, cannot grasp the soul that gives it life, the soul of the artist). Reading the catalog is a way to learn to recognize the soul that the artist has breathed into the work.

4. The theory of the automatic sweetheart is opposed to this way to approach art, which mainly applies to contemporary art, but is also widely present in more popular arts such as cinema, especially in the cultural phenomenon known as cinephilia. What is being asked of a work of art as an automatic sweetheart is primarily to function in itself, on its own, arousing emotions and thoughts regardless of the knowledge that the viewer might have about the author of the work. In ordinary experience, we meet people and we appreciate and judge them for *how they behave*, not for their noble birth; similarly, in artistic experience, we meet a work of art, i.e. an automatic sweetheart, and we appreciate and judge it for how it works, that is, for *how it seems to behave*.

The theory of the automatic sweetheart, in this respect, points out the possibility of a direct relationship with works of art, rather than mediated by the personality of the author. Here is the link with the idea of a "history of cinema without names": 'nameless', here, means above all 'authorless'. The primary interest is no longer given to the wires that move the puppet, and even less to the hand that pulls the wires; attention turns instead to the puppet itself, or the automatic sweetheart, regardless of the wires and hands that move it.

5. At this point, one should note that the theory of the automatic sweetheart is admittedly an incomplete theory of art. An automatic sweetheart is only a sufficient condition, not a necessary condition, to be a work of art. Namely, all works of art are automatic sweethearts, but there are also things that are automatic sweethearts without being works of art; for example, dolls, posters, Christmas trees, a security blanket, Winnicott's transactional objects, Christopher Lambert's speaking keychain in Marco Ferreri's *I love you* (cf. Terrone 2008).

The necessary condition that distinguishes works of art from other automatic sweethearts is to be found precisely in the importance of information on the history of the work's creation, in order to achieve an appropriate appreciation of the work itself. If one wants to properly appreciate and evaluate a work of art, one should not just treat it *as if it were a person*, but one must also know *what real person* has made it – in what historical context, within what cultural practice. The primary motivations that underlie the author's cult are not, therefore, totally unfounded; indeed, they individuate the additional component that allows one to narrow down the works of art within the wider set of automatic sweethearts.

6. The plurality of components of the artwork has been analyzed by Richard Wollheim (1980, 1998) in the specific case of pictures. Wollheim distinguishes three different levels of appreciation in the experience of a picture: (1) the "Recognitional Fold", which deals with recognizable scenes in the picture; (2) the "Configurational Fold", which concerns the material vehicle of the picture and the distribution of coloured marks on its surface; (3) The "Standard of Correctness" which regards the history of the picture's making and the intentions of the artist who created it.

The Configurational Fold is the joint that connects the Recognitional Fold to the Standard of Correctness: from the experience of the scenes depicted by an picture (Recognitional Fold), we can go back to the recognition of the author's intentions (Standard of Correctness) by means of the perceptual experience of the picture's surface as an object configured by the author (Configurational Fold). This is because the artist, according to his intentions (Standard of Correctness), configured the perceptible picture area (Configurational Fold) by which we recognize the depicted scenes (Recognitional Fold). Starting from this characterization, Wollheim argues that the proper appreciation of the picture consists in retracing the process of its creation; in this regard, he speaks of "criticism as retrieval", stating that "the task of criticism is the reconstruction of the creative process" (1980, 185).

7. Taking Wollheim's "criticism as retrieval" to its extreme consequences, the cult of the author focuses on the Standard of Correctness (what the artist "meant") treating the Configurational Fold (the experience of what the artist made) as the main object of attention, while relegating the Recognitional Fold (the experience produced by the artwork itself) to a secondary role. The cult of the author, therefore, underestimates the importance of the Recognitional Fold, placing too much emphasis on the Configurational Fold and on the Standards of Correctness.

Yet, as Wollheim himself makes very clear, the Standard of Correctness is an essential component of the picture: the cult of the author, to a certain extent, has a *raison d'être*. The work of art is an automatic sweetheart of which we also want to know the history of creation; a puppet of which we also want to see the wires, and even the puppeteer who moves them.

But the fact remains that the appreciation of the work of art as an automatic sweetheart, as a seemingly autonomous puppet, is a crucial moment of the aesthetic experience. And it is this aesthetic moment that is likely to be overshadowed by a conception of art focused on the author. There is a direct relationship with the work as an apparently autonomous individual, as an automatic sweetheart, which is preliminary to any appreciation of the work seen as the creation of a real person – the author, the artist. One should treat the work as if it were self-generated, and as if it were able to generate a number of experiences on its own: this is the main precept that follows from the theory of the work of art as an automatic sweetheart. In the particular case of cinema, this amounts to treating a film as a peculiar entity providing us with an experiential route through an objective world: namely, the world of the story told.

In this sense, the account of the film as an automatic sweetheart sharply differs from two important tendencies in the contemporary debate about cinema, namely, *intentionalism* and *illusionism*. According to *intentionalism*, recognizing the intentions of the filmmaker (either the real one, just as in cult of the author, or at least an implicit one) plays a fundamental role in our experience of films. According to *illusionism*, instead, our experience of fiction films has strong analogies with our embodied experience of the real world. On the one hand, intentionalism mainly draws on Gricean theories of communication (cf. Donati 2006, Kobow 2007) and on language-based cognitive science (cf. Pignocchi 2015). On the other hand, illusionism mainly draws on perception-based cognitive science (cf. Anderson 1996) and on neuroscience (cf. Gallese and Guerra 2015). Borrowing Wollheim's terminology, the focus on intentionalism is on the Configurational Fold and (through the "retrieval process") on the Standard of Correctness, whereas the focus of illusionism is on the Recognitional Fold understood as providing the spectator with an embodied perceptual access to the world depicted by the film, as if she had her own place in this world.

Our account sharply differs from intentionalism since we understand the film as an object that, at a basic level of appreciation, can be enjoyed as a generator of experiences, namely an automatic sweetheart, without the need to recognize the filmmaker's intentions. The recognition of intentions (through the Configurational Fold and the Standard of Correctness) allows us to add layers of appreciation and to enrich our experience of a film, but such an enrichment relies on a basic layer of appreciation in which we just treat the film as an automatic sweetheart independently of the filmmaker's intentions.

Still, our account also differs from illusionism since we do not treat the film as eliciting an embodied perceptual experience of the world depicted that is of the same kind as the ordinary perception of the actual world. Rather, according to our account, the spectator's experience basically concerns the film itself as an automatic sweetheart that supplies a *sui generis* disembodied perceptual experience of the world depicted. The film as an automatic sweetheart offers us a perceptual gift that is not normally available in our everyday experience.

As explained, treating the film as an automatic sweetheart does not prevent one from being also interested in the author and the context of production. The two dimensions of appreciation are complementary. First one appreciates the work as automatic sweetheart, then one looks into the wires and invisible hands moving her, and finally one goes back to treating her as if she were alive: aesthetic judgment is formed in this coming and going. Treating the work as an automatic sweetheart does not exhaust its appreciation, but is an indispensable key stage of the process.

8. In cultural practices, there is often a gap between two typical forms of appreciation: that "of the masses", who treat works primarily as automatic sweethearts; and that "of the experts", who treat the works as historical products of the artists who authored them. The point is that both of these modes of appreciation are limited. Therefore, the theory of the automatic sweetheart should not be confused with a revaluation of the mass-spectator understood as a noble savage who is not affected by cultural prejudices. On the other hand, the theory of the automatic sweetheart is also opposed to idealizing expert knowledge as a paradigm of the attitude that everyone should have towards artworks. More modestly, the theory of the automatic sweetheart tries to show that both these dimensions – the naïveté of the masses, the knowledge of the experts – play a key role in the appreciation of a work of art, as they both establish the identity of the work itself.

The ability to pretend to be a person identifies the *ontological genus* of works of art: that of automatic sweethearts. The essential link to the history of production and the author's creative activity identifies the *specific difference* of the artwork in relation to other automatic sweethearts. Therefore it is appropriate to treat a work of art as an automatic sweetheart because of the genus to which it belongs, but it is equally appropriate to take interest in the history of creation of the work because of its specific difference.

9. While both these aspects – automatic sweetheart and artist's creation – are essential to the understanding of the work of art, we believe that in the current historic phase the first aspect is usually underestimated compared to the second. This is what motivates us to interpret the project of a "history of cinema without names" (cf. Cavalotti, Giordano, Quaresima 2016) in terms of a history of films understood as automatic sweethearts.

Cinema and contemporary art have established themselves around the same period, roughly a century ago: Griffith's *The Birth of a Nation* dates 1915, and Duchamp's *Fountain* 1917. Yet their working mechanism seems profoundly different. The more cinema highlights the work as an automatic sweetheart, the more contemporary art enhances the work as the artist's emanation. Duchamp shows that any object can be a work of art, even a latrine, as long as the artist applies his signature, his name, to it. Griffith instead gives its audience a film as such capable of generating emotions, by virtue of the sheer force of its pictures, regardless of the author's name.

10. On closer inspection, however, the divide is not as clear as we have presented it so far. A film is also the result of the creative acts of an author, and a work of contemporary art is also an automatic sweetheart. In

particular, having now acquired legitimacy as an art form and not just as a form of entertainment, cinema recognizes directors as authors of films, and information about how a film was made imposes itself as an essential requirement for a proper appreciation of that film.

However, cinema has an inferiority complex *vis-à-vis* the traditional fine arts and their designated heir, contemporary art. This inferiority complex seems due to what Benjamin (1936) defines "aura". In the theoretical perspective of the automatic sweetheart we interpret the aura as the extra soul that the artist gives the work. The aura is to the artwork what the soul is to the body. That is, a work of art furnished with aura does not count as the disappointing automatic sweetheart of James's thought experiment; instead it counts as a real person.

That being the case, the loss of aura that characterizes cinema is not just about technical reproducibility, but especially about the ability to produce works – films – that may also function as automatic sweethearts without the need of a supplement of soul, of an aura. On the other hand contemporary art brings the idea of an aura to its extreme consequences, emphasizing the ability of artistic creation to transfigure the most miserable objects – Duchamp's latrine, Manzoni's shit – by infusing aura into them.

11. In a thought experiment concerning the nature of the work of art, Arthur Danto proposes to consider a curious character, unwilling to treat certain objects displayed in contemporary art museums as works of art: "Imagine, now, a certain Testadura – a plain speaker and noted philistine – who is not aware that these are art, and who takes them to be reality simple and pure" (1964, 575).

Danto's point is that Testadura lacks a proper theory of art, so he merely focuses on the observable properties of the works, without recognizing the hidden, unobservable ones: those related to the history of the work's creation, or to what we have defined as its aura – the extra soul that the artist has given it. At the contemporary art museum, Testadura only sees what is before him, failing to understand that it is a work of art and not an ordinary object. Seeing the beds exposed by Rauschenberg or Oldenburg, Testadura is tempted to lie down on them, and one can easily guess what would have occurred had he seen Duchamp's *Fountain*. Yet Testadura would not have such problems if he went to a theatre to watch a movie. This is because films present themselves as automatic sweethearts, and can be enjoyed without the need to grasp their aura.

12. This difference between cinema and contemporary art can be synthesized by means of a historical narrative. Until the nineteenth century, art appeared as a unitary phenomenon, such that the perceived appearance of the work and information about the history of its creation – in short, the automatic sweetheart on one side and the aura on the other – equally contributed to its appreciation. In the twentieth century, with the rise of cinema (and more generally of mass art, cf. Carroll 1998) and readymade art (and more generally of contemporary art), the unity of the artistic phenomenon split. On the one hand, cinema appears to be capable of offering automatic sweethearts without aura. On the other, contemporary art offers items, such as readymades, which are unable to function on their own as automatic sweethearts, and therefore require additional knowledge on the history of their creation, that is, the soul that the artist has breathed into them – the aura.

Until the nineteenth century, despite his limitations, Testadura could appreciate the works of art without any particular difficulty, and distinguish them from ordinary objects that clearly are not works of art. At most one could object to Testadura that his appreciation wasn't very deep, limited to observable qualities without taking into account the history of the work's creation; however, it could not be denied that Testadura's attitude towards the work of art was a genuine aesthetic appreciation. In the twentieth century, though, the art world was split in two: on one side the movie theatre that seems made for Testadura, on the other the contemporary art museum where Testadura gets lost in awkward misunderstanding.

It is noteworthy that the status of "work of art" has often been challenged both in the case of cinema and in that of readymade art, but for different reasons. In the case of films, the problem is the lack of aura; in the case of readymade art, the problem is that there is nothing but the aura. Simmetrically, one could say that in the case of readymade art the problem is that the automatic sweetheart seems to be missing, while in the case of films it seems to be all there is. In short, the film pleases Testadura too much to be a work of art, while the readymades don't please him enough.

In this paper we have tried to show that Testadura is not entirely in the wrong. There is a crucial dimension of aesthetic appreciation that is based on Testadura's naivety, and that means treating the work of art as something that looks like a person, as a generator of experiences, emotions and feelings – like an automatic sweetheart. In cinema this dimension is particularly prominent. A "history of cinema without names" can finally give it the importance it deserves.

Bibliographical References

Anderson J. D. (1996). *The Reality of Illusion: An Ecological Approach to Cognitive Film Theory*, Carbondale and Edwardsville, Southern Illinois University Press.

Benjamin, W (2008). *The Work of Art in the Age of Its Technological Reproducibility, and Other Writings on Media*. Boston, Harvard University Press.

Carroll, N. (1998). *A Philosophy Of Mass Art* (p. 102). Oxford, Clarendon Press.

Cavalotti D., Giordano F., Quaresima L., 2016, *A History of Cinema Without Names. A Research Project*, Milano, Mimesis International.

Danto, A. C. (1964). *The Artworld. The Journal Of Philosophy*, *61*(19), 571-584.

Danto, A. C. (1981). *The Transfiguration Of The Commonplace: A Philosophy Of Art*. Cambridge, Harvard University Press.

Donati, S. (2006). *Cinema e conversazione: l'interpretazione del film narrativo*, Civitavecchia, Prospettiva.

Ferraris, M. (2007). *La fidanzata automatica*, Milano, Bompiani.

Gallese, V., Guerra M. (2015), *Lo schermo empatico. Cinema e neuroscienze*, Milano, Cortina.

James, W. (1908). "The Pragmatist Account of Truth and Its Misunderstanders" The Philosophical Review XVII January 1908 (reprinted in *The Meaning of Truth*).

Kobow B. S. (2007). *See What I Mean – Understanding Films as Communicative Actions*, Paderborn, Mentis Verlag.

Pignocchi A. (2015), *Pourquoi aime-t-on un film? Quand les sciences cognitives discutent des goûts et des couleurs*, Paris, Odile Jacob.

Strawson, P. F. (1959). *Individuals*, London, Methuen.

Strawson, P. F. (1966). 'Aesthetic Appraisal and Works of Art', *The Oxford Review*, 3; reprinted in *Freedom and Resentment and Other Essays*, London, Methuen, 1974, pp. 178-188.

Terrone E. (2008) *Fidanzate in esubero* (Review of M. Ferraris, *La fidanzata automatica*), *Rivista di estetica*, n.s., n° 37, pp. 274-278.

Wollheim, R. (1980). *Art and its Objects*, Cambridge, Cambridge University Press.

Wollheim, R. (1998). *On Pictorial Representation. The Journal Of Aesthetics And Art Criticism*, *56* (3), 217-226.

REALISM

1.
REALISM AND TRANSPARENCY

1. *Varieties of realism*

Realism is spoken of in many ways. Speaking of realism, in fact, means dealing with the relationship between representations and reality, but depending on what you mean by "representation", and especially by "reality", you will have different notions of realism. In the case of cinematic representations, this polysemy of the term "realism" is articulated by Berys Gaut in seven different ways[1].

The first way could be defined *conceptual realism*, or verism, for which films are classified according to the truthfulness of the concepts necessary to understand them. A film is realistic if its understanding requires concepts that apply to our experience of reality: for example *Amour* (M. Haneke, 2012) is a realistic film because the concepts of old age, sickness, and death apply to reality, while *The Hobbit* (P. Jackson, 2012) is not because its understanding requires concepts such as those of hobbit or dragon, which are inapplicable to reality. Thus defined, conceptual realism is a very cursory notion that serves mostly to distinguish realist genres such as comedy and drama from anti-realist genres such as fantasy or science fiction. However, this concept of realism can be further clarified by also considering individual concepts, those that apply to single entities. In this way we can say for example that films such as *Lincoln* (S. Spielberg, 2012), *Argo* (B. Affleck, 2012) and *Zero Dark Thirty* (K. Bigelow, 2012), with their multiple references to facts that actually happened and individuals who really existed, are more realistic than movies like *Me and You* (B. Bertolucci, 2012) or *Silver Linings Playbook* (D.O. Russell, 2012). But it remains to be clarified what exactly concepts are, what content they have on a case-by-case basis, and in what precise sense they apply to reality or not; given the lack of agreement on these points, conceptual realism is reduced to a series of arbitrary choices.

---

1   B. Gaut, *A Philosophy of Cinematic Art*, Cambridge University Press, Cambridge 2010, pp. 60-97.

The second mode of realism is *illusionism*: making people believe that what they see is real, regardless of whether it is or not. While conceptual realism applies to any form of art, illusionism seems to capture a cinematic specificity, which refers to a foundational myth of the history of film: the legend by which spectators fled from the theatre when the train arrived at La Ciotat station. But the latter is indeed a myth, a hyperbolic figure – used as such by Welles in *Don Quixote* (1955) and Godard in *Les Carabiniers* (1963). In fact, cinematic viewers are almost never prey to an illusion that confuses the screen with reality. Illusionism therefore has a very limited explanatory power because it associates realism with a type of experience that is at most an exception, and which belongs to the domains of myth or fiction rather than to the field of reality.

The third mode of realism goes under the technical term of *photorealism*: the digital imitation of traditional photographic processes, the skillful use of special effects that makes films like *The Matrix* (L. and A. Wachowski, 1999) or *Avatar* (J. Cameron, 2009) realistic. Although the notion of photorealism applies only to digital cinema, it introduces a methodological novelty of fundamental importance: realism is no longer defined as the relationship between cinema and reality, but as the relationship between a certain type of cinema (the digital one) and another type of cinema (the analogue one). If we succeed in defining the realism of analogue cinema in terms of a relationship with a preexisting practice, we will have obtained a characterization of realism that does not require an ontological commitment on what exactly reality is. The search for this characterization leads to the notion of transparency which is the main theme of this essay. Before going into the matter, however, there are three classic conceptions of cinematic realism left to consider: ontological, epistemological and perceptual.

Ontological realism is a talent that cinema inherits from photography and consists in the ability to assert with absolute certainty: "this that I am showing you has really taken place". This conception finds its reference texts in Bazin's *Ontology of the Photographic Image*[2] and Barthes' *Camera Lucida*[3]. But what does "taken place" mean? And how can photography and cinema state with absolute certainty that "this has

---

2   A. Bazin, *Ontology of the Photographic Image*, tr. by Hugh Gray. Film Quarterly , Vol. 13, No. 4. (Summer, 1960), pp. 4-9.
3   R. Barthes, *Camera Lucida: Reflections on Photography*, New York, Farrar, Straus and Giroux 1981.

taken place"? Both Bazin and Barthes seem to assume that something that has "taken place" has occupied some portion of space-time, and that the "absolute certainty" of the photographic assertion derives from the direct causal relationship between this portion of space-time and the image. These metaphysical assumptions about space, time and causation, however, bind ontological realism to a materialist (or, at most, phenomenal) conception of reality, in relation to which epistemic realism and perceptual realism can be considered as amendments, or attempts to loosen these metaphysical bonds.

In particular, for *epistemic realism* it does not matter so much that a film tells us with absolute certainty "this has taken place", but rather that it gives us good reasons to believe it. In our culture, visual and sound recordings (especially analogue, less manipulative than the digital) are usually treated as reliable representations that, as far as we know about the techniques and practices with which they are produced, justify us in believing that what we see represented has actually happened. In this sense, photographs and films, unlike paintings and novels, play an important role in legal proceedings: therefore these representations are to be considered realistic because, according to our system of knowledge, they may act as clues and evidence.

Perceptual realism makes a move similar to that of epistemic realism – in that it relativizes ontological realism – but taking as a frame of reference not our system of knowledge but our perceptive system. A film is realistic to the extent that it works like perception. Since perception is an uninterrupted flow of images and sounds, a film shot in long take is more realistic than a film that uses montage. Or, to take another of Bazin's examples, visual perception smoothly puts space into focus in the direction of depth, so films that resort to deep focus are more realistic than those that blur the background as opposed to the figure.

Perceptual realism and epistemic realism are methodologically interesting for how they try to disengage themselves from an absolute notion of reality, respectively relating cinema with perception and knowledge. The problem is that both perception and knowledge are not unquestionably shared notions: they are rather the object of philosophical controversies that – although less harsh than those on the metaphysical status of reality – appear far from being resolved. With the aim of defining cinematic realism in terms of a relationship that does not involve reality as such, it would be useful to have a reference term that is easier to grasp than the notions of perception or knowledge. The theory of transparency is the way in which contemporary analytic aesthetics is trying to satisfy this need.

2. *The adventures of transparency*

The reference term needed to define realism without committing to the metaphysical status of reality consists of transparent surfaces such as windows, spyglasses and telescopes, or reflecting surfaces such as mirrors: in short, glass, in its many types and uses. The present overview, which started from the varieties of realism finds its point of arrival in transparency. The fundamental thesis of transparency theory is that cinema is realistic if it works like glass windows, telescopes, spyglasses, microscopes and mirrors. This correspondence takes place on a functional level: cinema can perform functions corresponding to those usually performed by visual devices such as mirrors and telescopes. Articulating the theory of transparency means addressing this functional correspondence: how exactly do transparent vision devices work? How exactly does cinema work? Do transparent devices and cinema really work the same way?

From a functional perspective, transparent vision devices have two crucial properties: *counterfactual dependence* and *indexicality*. A vision device like a telescope or a mirror shows us a certain fact; if the visual properties of this fact change significantly (thus constituting a *counter-fact*), what the device shows necessarily changes too, and counterfactual dependence consists precisely of this necessary link. Indexicality, instead, consists of the possibility of using transparent devices to directly *indicate* the object they show, to say for example "look at *this*!", as normally happens with the objects that are in front of us, using demonstrative pronouns that in semantics are classified as *indexical* terms. Given that counterfactual dependence and indexicality are the constitutive properties of transparent vision devices, if one can show that cinema has these two properties, it will be possible to characterize cinematic realism in terms of transparency.

To show that photographs and films have counterfactual dependence, Kendall Walton uses the example of an explorer who goes in search of a monstrous beast and eventually finds it[4]. If the explorer makes a drawing on a notebook, the drawing remains the same even in the counterfactual hypothesis that the beast does not really exist and our explorer has had

---

4   K. Walton, "Transparent Pictures: On the Nature of Photographic Realism", in Critical Inquiry, 11 (1984): 246–77.

a hallucination. But if the explorer shoots a film, then, if the beast is just one of his hallucinations, it will not appear in the film, just as it would not appear in a mirror. Thus films, like transparent devices, and unlike drawings and paintings, have the property of counterfactual dependence.

To show that films also have indexicality, we need to consider the nature of the relationship between representations and represented entities. In the case of the moving image, this relationship consists of a path that connects a film to its object preserving its visual properties (at least those needed to recognize it) through purely physical links, without the mediation of mental states such as beliefs, desires, or intentions. If the film is made with photographic techniques (analogue or digital), then the mental states of the creator can only determine what object is shown (just like the orientation of a telescope determines what star is observed), but not *how* it is shown, or what properties are attributed to it. In this sense, films function like telescopes or mirrors rather than as drawings or paintings: they create a direct path, devoid of mental mediations, between the observer and the represented object – they put them in *contact*, allowing the observer to use indexical pronouns such as "this" and "that" to refer to the object.

Such a contact, such a direct link between the observer and the object, which is at the basis of both counterfactual dependence and indexicality, is the fundamental characteristic that films share with transparent vision devices. It is because of this contact that films, like mirrors and telescopes, allow us to *see through*, that is, to perceive the object as if it were in front of us, even if in fact it is not. The rear-view mirror of a car reflects objects that are actually *behind* us and makes us see them *in front of* us. The telescope allows us to perceive in detail objects that are extremely distant from us, and which in some cases have even ceased to exist, such as stars imploded millennia ago that we continue to see because of the finiteness of the speed of light. Similarly, films work like rear-view mirrors where the "rear" is about time rather than space.

3. *Transparency and repetition*

The problem of transparency theory is that the way mirrors and telescopes work cannot be reduced to counterfactual dependence and indexicality[5].

---

5   For similar arguments against the transparency thesis see B. Gaut, *A Philosophy of Cinematic Art*, cit., pp. 78-97; and G. Currie, *Image and Mind: Film, Philosophy and Cognitive Science*, Cambridge University Press, Cambridge 1995, pp. 48-78.

There is a third property of transparent devices – location – which is equally essential for their functioning, but which cinema does not seem to have. Transparent devices allow the observer to *locate* in space the objects shown by the film, and consequently to orientate themselves with respect to these very objects. In other words, transparent devices support what is called a "situated vision": they make us see things that are in the same space as our body and with respect to which we can orientate ourselves. The window allows me to orientate myself with respect to the space that is outside of my room. The rearview mirror allows me to orientate myself with respect to the cars behind me. In a way, even a telescope that shows a star imploded millennia go allows me to orient myself with respect to that star: if I could time travel, I would know along which space-time path – along which ray of light – to go.

Cinema, on the other hand, does not allow for anything like that, it does not say anything about the relationship between the things shown and the spectator's body. The cinematic vision, in this sense, is "alienated"[6], "detached"[7]: films allow us to recognize things but not to orient ourselves in relation to them; they offer us a point of view but prevent our body from occupying it. It follows that cinema shares with transparent visual devices the properties of counterfactual dependence and of indexicality, but not the equally crucial property of location. So, films are not transparent to all effects, they are not entirely glass-like: their transparency is deteriorated by a "crack".

The theorists of transparency respond to this problem by noting that, on the one hand, some transparent devices do not allow you to locate your object (think of a submarine's periscope) and, on the other, that some moving images do provide a form of location (think of CCTV or video-entryphones)[8]. For example I can watch the webcam of my computer, instead of the mirror, when I shave in the morning: in this case the film image shows me a space in relation to which I can orient myself.

This defense strategy is not entirely convincing, because it focuses on peculiar empirical circumstances ignoring the range of possibilities that surrounds them. It is true that a sailor in a submarine cannot usually orient himself with respect to what he sees in a periscope, but he theoretically could do so if he had the possibility to go through the periscope tube

---

6   F. E. Sparshott, *Vision and Dream in the Cinema*, in "Philosophic Exchange", n. 1 (1975), p. 115.
7   N. Carroll, *Theorizing the Moving Image*, Cambridge University Press, Cambridge 1996, p. 62.
8   Cfr. A. Kanja, *Realism*, cit., pp. 241-242.

following the rays of light until he reached the object that reflected them. On the other hand, it's true that I can shave looking at the webcam instead of the mirror, but what I see on the computer screen is just a particular projection of a film, not the film. As a film, in fact, this morning's shaving is a sequence of images that can be projected in a number of different contexts. But if I used this same film to shave *tomorrow morning*, my body orientation with respect to the space depicted would fail miserably – on the screen I would see a serene morning shave; in front of the screen, there would be a bloodbath like the one in *The Big Shave* (M. Scorsese, 1967).

Location is therefore the main difference between transparent devices and cinema. But underlying location there is an ontological factor. Transparent devices like mirrors and telescopes proceed by singular ostensions: they show me a scene in its unrepeatable uniqueness, just as my eyes do. On the other hand, cinema is repeatable by nature: the scene that a film shows me can be seen in a variety of different contexts. This repeatability, however, is incompatible with location: in order to locate a scene and orientate myself around it I must be in an environment that is spatially and temporally connected with the environment in which the scene takes place, while the repeatability of cinema allows for the same scene to appear in any environment, regardless of the space-time connection between the projection environment and the shooting one.

Of course, there must also be a causal chain that leads from the so-called profilmic (through shooting, prints, copies, projection) to the image I am looking at. But this causal chain that connects the shot scene to the screened image is not a mere space-time path: it is not the path of a ray of light that, if I wanted, I could still retrace (through some very sophisticated technologies). This chain, in the case of films, is a historical process beyond the reach of any technology, a four-dimensional configuration of facts and objects that only a glance situated outside of our space-time – only God's point of view – would allow us to retrace step by step, in reverse. So movies do not work like glasses and mirrors, and cinematic realism does not offer us the same perceptual access to things as glasses and mirrors.

The transparency theory, like its predecessors, fails to provide a fully satisfactory account of cinematic realism. But it is a glorious failure, a honorable defeat. On the one hand, in fact, the theory of transparency reveals that films work like mirrors at least as regards counterfactual dependence and indexicality: films, like glass and mirrors, significantly put us in contact with the scenes depicted. On the other hand, the transparency theory, precisely because of its failure, reveals in what way the contact that a film establishes between the scene and the image differs from that established by glasses and mirrors: a film does not allow for the location of the objects and consequently not even for the spectator's orientation inside the scene depicted; however, it allows us to repeat the vision of this same scene at will.

The contact between the spectator and the scene, in the case of cinema, is a defective one, a cracked transparency: it has counterfactual dependence and indexicality, but the possibility of location and orientation is missing. This defect depends on the fact that cinema reifies vision, transforming it into a repeatable structure that interposes itself between the spectator and the scene. It is therefore a defect that can be reversed into a merit. The break of transparency is the price that cinema pays to emancipate the perceptive experience from its absolute singularity and its congenital finiteness.

2.
WHAT'S NEW IN REALISM?
Philosophy and Cinema Rediscover Reality

"New realism" is a philosophical movement developed in Italy since the publication of Maurizio Ferraris's book *Manifesto del nuovo realismo* in 2011[1]. The present contribution aims to settle the debt that philosophical realism has with its illustrious cinematic antecedent. First of all (§§ 1-5), we will characterize the historical novelty that both realisms carry in their name as a reaction to political and cultural structures that have stubbornly belittled reality: twenty years of fascism in the case of neorealism, and twenty years of Berlusconi in the case of new realism. Then (§§ 6-7), we will highlight the structural link between neorealism and new realism, making use of the Aristotelian distinction between *mythos* and *historìa*. On the one hand, philosophical new realism defends a conception of reality as *historìa* that resists *mythos*. On the other hand, cinematic neorealism opposes the closure of narration into pure *mythos*, opening it instead in the direction of *historìa*.

1. Neorealism arose in Italy at the end of Mussolini's "long" two decades (1922-1943); new realism, at the end of Berlusconi's "short" two decades (1994-2011). These two periods have significant similarities but also decisive differences. Probably the most enlightening way to compare them is Marx's famous note in chapter one of *The Eighteenth Brumaire of Louis Bonaparte*: "Hegel remarks somewhere that all great world-historic facts and personages appear, so to speak, twice. He forgot to add: the first time as tragedy, the second time as farce."

A similar argument applies to the relationship between cinematic neorealism and philosophical new realism. The first is basically the reaction to a tragedy; the second, the reaction to a farce. Yet, beyond the obvious differences of scope and merit, neorealism and new realism seem to have something essential in common: they are both reactions to

---

1   M. Ferraris, *Manifesto del nuovo realismo*, Rome-Bari 2011.

times dominated by the devaluation of objective reality. In this sense, it is interesting to note that both these forms of realism feel the need to connote themselves as "new". It is not only a matter of affirming realism, but of affirming it as opposed to a hegemonic culture that had suspended its relationship with reality.

The dominant philosophy in Italy during the Fascist era was the neo-idealism of Croce and Gentile, while the dominant philosophy in the Berlusconi era was postmodernism based on the "hermeneutic and emancipatory" reinterpretations of Nietzsche and Heidegger (curiously, the Nazis' favourite philosopher and the philosopher who sympathized with the Nazis). Although neo-idealism and postmodernism are very different philosophical orientations, they share a hegemonic attitude towards reality. In Croce's Hegelian idealism, reality is resolved in the manifestation of the spirit in history; in Gentile's Fichtean idealism, reality is only the result of the subject's thought. Similarly, for postmodernism reality is reduced to the result of interpretation practices: the banner of postmodernists in this sense is Nietzsche's note in his *Posthumous Fragments*: "facts are just what there aren't, there are only interpretations".

2. Unlike Plato, who never saw the realization of his philosophical state, postmodernists had to see all their projects implemented rather quickly. But it was not necessarily a privilege. Let us take the first and most important of postmodernist assumptions – universally shared from German anarchist epistemologists to French post-structuralists, from American neo-pragmatists to Italian weak thinkers – namely the idea that truth and reality, the reference to an external world, are violent and despotic notions of little practical use and even more dubious theoretical defensibility, since there is no external world to refer to.

In this trial against the outside world, postmodernists manifested a sincere emancipatory will: truth and reality are cumbersome and binding notions, the point is to reach beyond them, just as beyond metaphysics and of course science. Considering the importance of truth and reality within everyday practices, one would think that such a vast design had very little chance of implementing itself. And yet it is precisely what happened, for example when engineer Castelli, the Minister of Justice for the second Berlusconi government, had the words "the law is the same for all" (legal equivalent of the thesis that reality and the truth are the same for everyone) replaced with "justice is administered in the name of the people" (demagogic version of the Nietzschean motto "facts are just what there aren't, there are only interpretations").

A second conceptual core of postmodernism – following the decline of truth – was the idea of not adhering entirely to one's own beliefs, and of presenting oneself as an "ironic theorist" who does not fully believe what one says and does. Again, the underlying inspiration was genuinely emancipating and non-violent: religious wars are triggered by fanatics who are all too convinced of their beliefs, better take things with greater detachment. But then this wish came true, so to speak, with populist leaders governing with jokes, offering the (perverse or perfect?) incarnation of the "ironic theorist" described by Rorty as a desirable future for democracy. Here is a new and unexpected meaning for the motto "a laughter that will bury you all". Who could have thought that one day we would be ruled by comedians?

As Boileau put it in *Art Poétique*, "Laissons à l'Italie / De tous ces faux brillants l'éclatante folie". And yet this prompt and unexpected realization has also taken place in another field, that of sexual liberation. It was the third programmatic point of postmodernism, proposed by Deleuze and Guattari with the project of a "desiring revolution". Now, thirty year later, sexual deconstruction has become the rule even among those who did not read Deleuze, indeed, more so for them (for example the heroes of reality shows) than for others (the readers of *Anti-Oedipus*, who meanwhile have aged and become professors). Obviously, once again the realization of the dream involved a slight perversion, since sexual emancipation did not correspond in the least to a political liberation. It was rather like what the philosophers of the Frankfurt School called "repressive desublimation", illustrating the concept with William II's saying that the absolute ruler can act undisturbed so long as his subjects have a park in which to have free sexual encounters.

3. The fact that populism fulfills the dreams of postmodernism is the demonstration that the latter captured something real. But postmodernists do not seem to have been at all satisfied with this realization. Oscar Wilde said that there is only one thing worse than not realizing one's aspirations: namely realizing them. This is what happens with the primacy of interpretation, irony or sexual liberation: we love fairy tales (especially as children), but we would not like to see them as news on TV. We appreciate the figure of an old ironic professor who distributes his knowledge without presumption, but we do not expect that a politician-Père Ubu who turns everything into farce may end up being the worst absolutist. We understand the political importance of sexual emancipation, but we do not imagine that there can be sexual freedom in a climate *à la* Ancien Régime.

Perhaps the most realistic position is that of Slavoj Žižek: postmodernism was a good prophet, even if the prophecy itself was not positive, in that it anticipated the social and political perversions that underlie populism. However, to think that philosophical postmodernism is the best way to explain media populism is a little like thinking that only the sick can understand the sick. Which is correct, in an abstract sense: the sick do understand the sick. But the problem is that they are also very likely to justify them. Whereas, again, the postmodernist philosopher is not at all inclined to justify the media populist: indeed, he is a radical critic of the latter.

4. Philosophical new realism arises in reaction to such a deviation of postmodernism. If postmodernists were faced with a compact and granitic reality (even only ideologically) and felt the need to deconstruct it, new realism notes that we are faced with an antithetical process, that is, a deeply deconstructed reality, one that, as it were, is de-legitimized *qua* reality. Therefore, it is from reality that we should start again, because if we do not have reality and truth it is unclear how we can find the difference between transforming the world and simply believing to transform it, or dreaming of transforming it. It is truly hard to understand how it is possible to sustain *at the same time* that (1) reality does not exist, (2) we must say farewell to the truth, and (3) we need to transform the world. It is a bit like Freud's kettle: a man lends a kettle to another, who gives it back broken, and replies that he had returned the kettle undamaged, that it was already damaged when he borrowed it, and that he had never borrowed the damn kettle in the first place.

Now, Derrida has often made a very important point, namely that justice is the indeconstructible, meaning that all the dismantling, unmasking, and deconstructing, in fact, was animated by the search of justice. And at the same time he suggested that all the dismantling could not go so far as to touch justice, as in the cynicism by which that request for justice would hide other arguments, less clean and confessable.

And this is indeed the crux of the matter: what makes something just if not, ultimately, truth and reality? And yet truth and reality are precisely what philosophical postmodernism and media populism chose to leave behind. Precisely because there is a solid and unamendable world, impervious to our manipulations and interpretations, can there be something like justice. After all, it is simply a question of not believing the easy sophistry that being realistic means accepting the existing state of things. It is like thinking that a judge who is ascertaining the truth is thereby accepting it. What else can be offered as a philosophical and political alternative, in a world sick of fairy tales, if not reality?

5. This is where the connection between philosophical new realism and cinematic neorealism becomes substantial. Fascist cinema, between white telephones and iron crowns, was sick of fairy tales. This does not mean underestimating its aesthetic qualities, but only recognizing that its relationship with reality was significantly deteriorated. In this sense, we can compare the diversional function that cinema played in the Fascist era to the diversional function of television shows of the Berlusconi era (see the illuminating sequence on "Casa Vianello" and "Non è la Rai" in the TV series *1992*, which addresses the genesis of Berlusconism).

In short, both cinematic neorealism and philosophical new realism are *new* in the sense that they propose realism as a way out of an era in which the relationship with reality turned out to be suspended due to a sort of spell. Of course, there is the important difference that in one case it is a question of cinematic realism, in the other of philosophical realism. And yet, these two elements have an important trait in common: the attention to the irreducible singularity of events, places and individuals, in contrast to the attempt to reduce reality to nothing more than an arbitrary construction, a game of interpretations, a fairy tale.

6. This leads us to the structural distinction that we consider decisive to understand what unites cinematic neorealism and philosophical new realism, understood as cultural reactions to the political era that preceded them. It is the Aristotelian distinction between *mythos*, a discourse that subordinates reality to the story, and *historìa*, a discourse that instead undertakes to follow reality in its multiple individualities and facets. Realism, in cinema as in philosophy, is the choice of *historìa*.

On the first level, the distinction between *mythos* and *historìa* corresponds to the distinction between the narration of fictitious events (in which we can include epic, tragedy, comedy, drama, in all possible versions – theatrical, literary, cinema...) and the narration of real events (which includes history books and biographies, documentaries, etc.). In the *Poetics* Aristotle states that *mythos* talks about the universal and the necessary, while *historìa* deals with the particular and the contingent, and draws the conclusion that, for this reason, *mythos* must be considered superior to *historìa*.

This conclusion may seem to contrast with the ontological conception that Aristotle himself proposed in the *Categories*, according to which what exists in the primary sense are particular and contingent individuals (the "first substances"), not universal and necessary structures (the Platonic ideas, which Aristotle criticizes and traces back to "secondary substances", ontologically dependent on first substances). The point is that, according to Aristotle, although reality is made up of individuals, human knowledge concerns universals (species, genres, categories). Therefore, if art has a cognitive function, *mythos* should be preferred over *historìa*.

In drawing this conclusion, however, Aristotle seems to presuppose that the knowledge provided by art must be of the same type as that provided by science and philosophy. Nevertheless, the situation changes significantly if we consider that art is able to provide us with a peculiar knowledge of reality, precisely by virtue of a privileged relationship with the particular and contingent dimension of *historìa*. This knowledge of reality is one where the universal is known by coming into contact with the particulars that exemplify it. This is where new realism and neorealism meet.

On the one hand, new realism proposes a strongly *historìa*-oriented conception of the world: a world inhabited by particular individuals at the mercy of contingent events. On the other hand, neorealism maintains an essential link with *historìa*: it is the attempt to bring as much *historìa* as possible into the domain of *mythos*. Although neorealist films are still fictionals non-documentary films, and in this sense fall into the domain of *mythos*, they are however oriented to the dimension of the particular and of the contingent characteristic of *historìa*. This happens both at the level of staging, with outdoor shooting and non-professional actors, and at the level of the script, with narrative constructions sensitive to openings and digressions. This is the idea of neorealism that André Bazin sums up masterfully when, speaking of the fourth episode of *Paisà*, he writes "The camera, as if making an impartial report, confines itself to following a woman searching for a man, leaving to us the task of being alone with her, of understanding her, and of sharing her suffering"[2] This is also the idea that Gilles Deleuze (1989) developed talking about "pure optical and sound situations" in which the character itself escapes the diktat of the script: "the characters were found less and less in sensory-motor 'motivating' situations, but rather in a state of strolling, of sauntering or of rambling"[3].

This "French" way of reading neorealism as a penetration of *historìa* into the domain of *mythos* is contrasted by the brilliant analysis of an English scholar, Christopher Wagstaff. In *Italian Neorealist Cinema: An Aesthetic*

---

2   A. Bazin, *What Is Cinema?*, Berkeley: University of California Press, 2004 (Original French Edition: *Qu'est-ce que le cinéma?*, Paris: Éditions Du Cerf, 1958-62), pp. 36-37.

3   G. Deleuze, *Cinema 2 The Time Image*, University of Minnesota Press, 1989 (Original French Edition: *Cinéma 2. L'Image-temps*. Paris: Minuit, 1985), p. 120.

Approach (2007)[4], Wagstaff warns us against treating the masterpieces of neorealism as if they were nothing more than *historìa*, showing how the dimension of *mythos* is crucial to their understanding. Still, the *mythos* of neorealist films is somewhat different from the paradigmatic cases of *mythos* (for example the classical tragedies referred to by Aristotle in *Poetics*), and this peculiarity seems to derive precisely from the proximity that neorealism establishes between *mythos* and *historìa*. Of course, it can be shown, as Wagstaff does masterly, that neorealist films have a notable aesthetic relevance regardless of their link with historical reality. However, if one disregards their link with historical reality, something crucial for their appreciation seems to be irretrievably lost. Although neorealist films perfectly work also as instances of *mythos*, their full value can only be grasped by considering the connection that they establish between *mythos* and *historìa*. This value is both aesthetic and ontological: it cannot be appreciated as aesthetic if we do not recognize it above all as ontological.

7. In conclusion, cinematic neorealism and philosophical new realism are united by the priority accorded to *historìa* as opposed to *mythos*, in contrast to philosophical and political regimes (idealism and Fascism on the one hand, postmodernism and Berlusconism on the other) that instead sought to replace *historìa* with *mythos*. Of course, to take its revenge on *mythos*, *historìa* does not need to wait for cinema or philosophy. A war or a financial crisis can be more than enough. Cinema and philosophy can, however, in their small way, make a choice between *mythos* and *historìa*. Although in very different times and ways, neorealism and new realism have both chosen *historìa*.

---

4   Ch. Wagstaff, *Italian Neorealist Cinema: An Aesthetic Approach*, University of
      Toronto Press, 2007. Another account of neorealism that highlights its mythos
      dimension, as well as its ideological underpinnings, is that proposed by Gaspare
      De Caro in his outstanding book *Rifondare gli italiani? Il cinema del neorealismo*,
      Jaca Book 2014.

TECHNOLOGY

1.
THE FILM LIBRARY OF BABEL

Starting from a cinematic reinterpretation of Borges's *Library of Babel*, I attempt to provide a new answer to the old ontological question: "What kind of object is a film?". This answer, which takes into account the changes brought by the digital era, is developed through a comparison with Carroll's philosophy of motion pictures. While discussing, criticizing and trying to complete his theory, I will examine the concept of film under four different aspects: as a material object, as an ideal object, as an object of experience, and as a social object. Finally, this ontological account will be applied to clarify some traditional theoretical dualisms: i.e. film versus reality, film versus narration, film versus discourse, film versus art.

1. *Babel*

The Film Library (which some improperly call the Universe) consists of a huge number of projection rooms. The rooms are located in a multistory building, they are soundproofed and arranged along large corridors. Each room includes twenty five seats, five per row, a projector and a screen. In each room the same film is projected at regular intervals, with a maximum duration of three hours. Each film is projected at 24 frames per second. Each frame consists of 8,847,360 light dots, distributed over 2160 rows and 4096 columns; each light dot has a colour that varies in a range of 68.719.476.736 possible values. Each film is synchronized with a soundtrack, formed by a series of sound samples, with a cadence of 96,000 samples per second; each sound sample varies in a range of 16,777,216 possible values.

There are three fundamental characteristics that describe the Film Library. First: the Film Library contains a huge, but finite and calculable, number of films. Second: the Film Library has no two identical films. Third: all the films of history exist in the Film Library (although films lasting more than three hours are divided into portions projected in different rooms), together

with those that will be filmed in the future, as well as all the films that could
have been produced but have not been completed. The sum of these sets,
however, is only an infinitesimal part of the contents of the Film Library.

These principles have allowed for a general theory of the Film Library
and for a definition of its essential problem: the shapeless and chaotic nature
of almost all the films. Some of them are reminiscent of the noise signal
that appears on TV when the antenna is not connected. Others are simple
labyrinths of dots and noises, in which, however, one can occasionally
glimpse geometrical figures or listen to phonemes of Indo-European
languages. For every recognizable image, for any sensible word, there are
legions of tedious absurdities, of audiovisual jumbles and inconsistencies.

On the other hand, the Film Library is total, and its rooms contain all
the possible combinations of images and sounds, that is, all that can be
expressed in visual and auditory form. Everything: the entire production
of silent cinema, where every copy without sound corresponds to a
large quantity of variations with musical arrangements, scene noises
and dialogues dubbed in all languages; the entire production of sound
cinema; the entire production of amateur, high and low-definition videos;
the entire television production, including newscasts, commercials and
live coverage of all historical events, even those that existed before the
invention of cinema.

When it was discovered that the Film Library included all the films
in the world, the first reaction was one of extraordinary happiness. All
people felt like the masters of a secret treasure. At that time there was
much talk of "Vindications": apologetic and prophetic films that forever
reproduced the deeds of each person in the universe and appeared as
prodigious mysteries for his or her future: in these works the most
significant moments of a person's life – from birth to death, from the
happiest moments to the most tragic ones – were carefully selected and
assembled, enclosing one's existence in a story. Thousands of ambitious
people searched the Film Library, driven by the vain purpose of finding
their own Vindication. These pilgrims squabbled in the corridors, uttered
obscure threats, fought on the stairways, destroyed the projectors that
were screening deceptive films. Many went mad … Vindications do
exist and some claim to have grasped a few fragments in otherwise
incomprehensible films, but the probability of finding one's own
Vindication, or some perfidious variant of it, is substantially null.

Excessive hope, as natural, was followed by excessive depression. The certainty that some room concealed a precious film and that this room was inaccessible seemed almost intolerable. A blasphemous sect suggested that research be interrupted and that all people should mix images and sounds until these canonical films were made by an unlikely gift of chance. Others, on the other hand, believed that the important thing was to get rid of useless films: to their hygienic, ascetic fury, we owe the senseless devastation of millions of rooms. Their name is excommunicated, but those who desperately seek the "treasures" that their frenzy destroyed are neglecting two obvious facts. First: the Film Library is so enormous that any human reduction will be infinitesimal. Second: each piece is unique, irreplaceable, but (as the Film Library is total) there are always billions of imperceptibly imperfect variations, that is, films that do only differ for a colour nuance in a single point of a single frame.

2. *From the Film Library to the ontology of film*

This impertinent paraphrase of Borges's *Library of Babel* is based on the numerical values of the "4K" standard, which is currently the most advanced frontier of digital cinema, able to guarantee an audiovisual quality comparable, if not superior, to the traditional 35mm film[1]. Keeping the abstract and total space of the Film Library as a reference, in what follows I will try to answer the question: what kind of object is the film? In particular, in the second paragraph, I will explain how the advent of the digital format, with its Babelic implications, signifies the ultimate crisis of the traditional (and etymological) identification between film and its material support. In the third paragraph, I will put forward the hypothesis that the film – as an element of the Film Library – can be treated as an ideal object, comparable to the abstract entities of mathematics and linguistics. In the fourth paragraph, I will show how a more precise definition, one that would bring some order in the Babelic chaos of the Film Library, must necessarily take into account the cognitive performance of the viewer, and therefore involve a definition of the film as an object of experience. In the fifth paragraph, I will move from the definition of the film as an object of experience to its inclusion in the field of social objects, which finally makes it possible to extract the film from the abstract space of

---

1   In retrospect, the analogue becomes a sub-case of the digital just as mute cinema became a sub-case of sound film.

the Film Library and return it to the historical world. Finally, in the sixth paragraph, I will propose a unitary conception film that takes into account its different ontological dimensions (material, ideal, psychological, social) and, starting from there, I will try to deduce and discuss the four main functions (evidential, narrative, discursive, artistic) that have historically been assigned to films.

3. *The downfall of film as a material object*

The most immediate theoretical implication of the digital revolution is that cinema has shifted from the autographic to the allographic domain. According to the taxonomy of artistic practices introduced by Nelson Goodman (1968: 91-110), arts like painting and sculpture are *autographic*, in that they can be considered as "autographs" of the author, inextricable from the singularity of creation and affected by the notions of signature, authenticity and falsification. On the other hand, arts like music and literature are *allographic*, in that they feature a notation that allows to encode the work freeing it from material contingencies and thwarting the distinction between original and fake (a fake is in fact an object that pretends to have the same genesis as the original, while notation emancipates the work from its production). Goodman then introduces a second distinction – transversal to the previous one – between one-stage arts, where the work is concluded directly by the author, and two-stage arts, where instead further processing takes place (interpretation for music, performance for theatre, printing for engraving). The result is a scheme like this:

	One-stage	*Two-stage*
Autographic	Painting, sculpture	Engraving
Allographic	Literature	Music, theatre

Goodman does not explicitly deal with cinema, which however – in its traditional analogical form – easily falls back to the case of engravings, considering the original negative as the first stage (cliché) and the distributed copies as the second stage (prints). Analogic cinema is therefore a two-stage autographic art, which contemplates the author's will to sign a work (think of Hitchcock's habit of appearing in each of his films) and the possibility of falsifying it (one can well shoot a fake *Notorious* with the look-alikes of Cary Grant and Ingrid Bergman; likewise, there were several fake versions of Méliès' *A Trip to the Moon* circulating in the United States after 1902). It remains to be noted that the technical reproducibility implied by the "two stages" makes the work less bound to the singularity and the material contingency of its genesis[2]: a cinematographic work continues to exist even if the original negative is destroyed, just as a print survives even if the cliché may have been destroyed (on condition that at least one copy survives), while a destroyed painting is permanently lost.

The advent of digital technologies takes the emancipation of the work from materiality to the extreme, and realizes what Goodman (1968: 220) characterizes as the overcoming of the primordial autographic stage of the art, providing cinema with a notation that releases film from its particular production. With digital cinema, it no longer makes sense to talk about signatures and fakes: if I can make a digital film composed of the same series of pixels as the 4k version of *Notorious*, I will not produce a "fake *Notorious*" but the real one, exactly as Pierre Menard rewrote *Don Quixote*, finding it in the library of Babel in the same position in which Cervantes had found it.

The notation that makes cinema migrate from the autographic village to the allographic metropolis has a peculiarity in relation to the corresponding notations of music and literature: the digital code is completely extraneous to both the artist's practice and the spectator's experience. In literature the knowledge of the notation is a necessary condition both for the creation and for the appreciation of the work, and in music it can significantly benefit both. However, as far as digital cinema is concerned, it is not possible

---

2   The passage of the autographic work from the "single stage" to the "double stage" is implicitly dealt with in Walter Benjamin's famous essay *The Work of Art in the Age of Mechanical Reproduction*, based on the reversal of the traditional question "Is cinema art?" into its opposite: "Is art cinema?" (that is, is art part of a broader framework of production of social objects, within which the artistic function can coexist with others?). In arguing in favour of this overturning, Benjamin uses two quotes from Paul Valéry that could have been written today. The first is: "For the last twenty years neither matter nor space nor time has been what it was from time immemorial. We must expect great innovations to transform the entire technique of the arts, thereby affecting artistic invention itself and perhaps even bringing about an amazing change in our very notion of art." (1935: 1). The second is: "Just as water, gas, and electricity are brought into our houses from far off to satisfy our needs in response to a minimal effort, so we shall be supplied with visual or auditory images, which will appear and disappear at a simple movement of the hand, hardly more than a sign." (1935: 2).

for a director to create the entire film by sequencing numbers[3], nor can a spectator understand something of a film by reading it digit by digit. The numerical coding concerns the recording, transmission and preservation of the film, while it has little to do with the creative act and nothing to do with the perceptual phase.

The notation of literature is the language of literature just as the notation of music is the "language" of music (scare quotes are imposed by the indeterminacy of the semantic dimension), while the digital code is not the language of cinema, with or without scare quotes. In fact, cinema does not have its own specific language, but only a repertoire of expressive practices[4].

4. *The rise of film as an ideal object*

The existence of a notation brings allographic arts closer to the domain of mathematical entities, which for realist philosophies constitute the paradigm of ideal objects. The classic Goodmanian distinction can therefore be read – as Peter Kivy (2002: 243-269) does – in terms of a distinction between works that consist of material objects (autographic) and works that consist of ideal objects (allographic): "The reason one can steal the Mona Lisa and not Beethoven's Fifth Symphony is that the Mona Lisa is a physical object and Beethoven's Fifth Symphony is a... *What is it*? That is the question" (2002: 202). Kivy's answer is based on the striking analogy between numbers and musical works (2002: 209), namely on the fact that "The analogy between Beethoven's Fifth and the number two holds perfectly, at least as far as we have taken it: neither can be stolen and neither can be sold; and, of course, there are a great many other things we can't do to the number two and to Beethoven's Fifth Symphony, all

---

3   At most, the artist uses high level instructions, similar to those found in the programming language Alice to create and animate "visual worlds" (Cooper, Dann, Pausch 2006); but these instructions are based on "primitive" images whose conception is not reducible to the code.

4   The linguistic conception of cinema has been vigorously opposed by George M. Wilson (2006: 91-99) and rigorously refuted by Gregory Currie (2006: 287-298) and by Noël Carroll (2008: 102-108). Cinema uses language (both spoken and written) but is not in itself a language, unless you want to treat things and images of things in the same way as words, following the example of the Lagado Academics in *Gulliver's Travels*.

apparently due to the fact that neither is a physical object, locatable in space and time" (2002: 210).

Where these objects *can* be located Kivy does not explicitly say, but he draws a very original conclusion: if musical works are ideal objects that exist outside of space-time and therefore exist – always have, always will (2002: 212), then it is not possible to create them but only to discover them. What common sense calls "creation" is simply the first tokening, which reveals the work, the discovery to the world (2002: 215).

Kivy's argument can be extended from music to all allographic arts, and the library of Babel identifies this "abstract space" where all the works have existed forever and ever, and within which the artist makes his discoveries (in this sense, Pierre Menard would simply be an explorer who arrived after Cervantes, just as Vespucci arrived after Columbus).

Allographic arts therefore produce works that, by virtue of their reducibility to a formal notation, can be interpreted as ideal objects, located within a Multimedia Library of Babel, or in an all-encompassing abstract space, within which artistic creation is explained in terms of discovery. Allography involves the presence of a notation, and every notation tends to a Babel-like proliferation. The implications of the digital revolution are thus better clarified: cinema passes from the autographic to the allographic domain, the film moves from the field of material objects to that of ideal objects, and filmmaking comes down to the discovery of an entity that has always existed within the film library of Babel.

5. *The definition of the film as an object of experience*

The problem of every Library of Babel is the "shapeless and chaotic" nature of almost all its elements. The theorist who aims to provide a more appropriate definition of form of art is forced to behave like the sect of fundamentalists who get rid of useless texts, scouring the halls of the library with an ascetic fury, hoping to obtain a subset only composed of "well formed" works.

In the linguistic field, a first significant reduction of the library is imposed by grammatical rules, which allow one to select the "well formed" sequences extracting them from the totality of the possible combinations of symbols. In the musicological field, the classic example of a subset of the Babelic chaos is the tonal system, which in fact lends itself to being schematized through the rules of generative linguistics (Jackendoff and Lerdahl 1983).

In cinema, many historically established theories can be interpreted as implicit attempts to reduce the complexity of the film library of Babel. Among these, the contribution that best accounts for the theoretical turn imposed by the digital format comes from Noël Carroll (2006: 113-134 and 2008: 53-79). Carroll's decisive move is recognizing that the object of experience is independent from the specificity of the medium that supports it. Insisting on the ontological relevance of the lexical difference between film (recording medium) and movie (the outcome of the screening)[5], one might say that the classical ontologies of cinema (Bazin, Kracauer, Cavell) have tried to define it by focusing on the film, when it should have been defined by focusing on the movie. In fact, material media are historically determined and therefore transitory[6].

If the film is something that can be recorded onto a heterogeneous plurality of surfaces, what bears a film's particular features is not the medium but the inscription itself, and above all the experience it makes possible. On this basis, Carroll identifies five conditions necessary to define a film as a "moving image":

1) "detached display", so that the space of the screening is detached from the spectator's;
2) the possibility of the impression of movement;
3) the performance-token (screenings) of the work-type are generated by a template (the support) which is in turn a token (i.e. a copy);
4) the performance-token (the screening) is not as such a work of art;
5) bidimensionality.

To what extent do these five necessary conditions allow us to find our way in the Film Library of Babel? (1) and (5) are essential characteristics

---

5   This difference is suggested by a verse of Counting Crows' song, "Miss Potter's Lullaby": "If dreams are like movies, then memories are films about ghosts".

6   In supporting his thesis, Carroll highlights the two-stage autographic nature of cinema and its transition to allography: "One might think that the master or negative is privileged. But the negative of Murnau's *Nosferatu* was destroyed [...] and yet *Nosferatu* survives. Indeed, all the prints can be destroyed and the film will survive if a laser disc does, or if a collection of photos of all the frames does, or if a computer program of it does whether on disc, or tape or even on paper or in human memory."(2006: 128). To clarify the concept, Carroll (2006: 133) refers to the final scene of *Fahrenheit 451*, imagining a community within which, instead of the words, people memorize the numerical codes of films.

of any film of the Library which, regardless of its being "well formed" or "badly formed", will always be "detached" and "two-dimensional" (we could add: rectangular or otherwise inscribed in a rectangle, delimited by a beginning and an end, and synchronized with a soundtrack)[7].

(3) and (4), based on the type / token pair, serve to distinguish cinema from theatre and mean that the theatrical representation gives an added value to the original text while the film screening doesn't (but what about the proverbial pianist in silent movies?). To the objection that two-dimensionality would suffice to distinguish cinema from theatre, Carroll responds with the counterexample of shadow puppetry, which is two-dimensional and yet belong to theatre, not cinema; in this case, however, what is really decisive is not the type / token pair, but the fact that film is a recording (consisting of a given number of frames per second) while shadow puppetry is represented live; replacing conditions (3) and (4) with the postulate of recording also allows to exclude live television from the list of films[8], which would contradict condition (1) about detached vision in the case in which the spectator is indeed the person who is being filmed. However, not even the postulate of recording is enough in the chaos of the Film Library, where every film is recorded, regardless of its formal correctness. The only really useful condition for discriminating "well-formed" films is the one found in point (2) and that Carroll explicitly takes from Arthur C. Danto's essay *Moving Pictures* (1979): "the possibility of the impression of movement".

Danto's condition is based on the literal meaning of the term *movie*: "Moving pictures are just that: pictures which move, not just (or necessarily at all) pictures of moving things." (1979: 108). But what exactly does it mean that picture moves? If by picture we mean the rectangle projected on the screen, the movement of the picture would involve the movement of this rectangle on the walls of the room, which is not exactly the show that you expect to see when you go to the cinema (if it happens, it means the projector is broken or the projectionist doesn't know how to operate it). The movement does not concern the referent of the image either (if that were the case, notes Danto, Bruegel's pictures would also be films) or

---

7   Even silent films have their own soundtrack, that is, typically, silence, as evidenced by the fact that if someone is chatting during the screening of a silent film, the other spectators get angry.

8   In live television, unlike in the case of shadow puppetry, you can still speak if not of recording, at least of transcription: the sounds and images, to be sent elsewhere, must be transcribed (i.e. transformed into a series of frames synchronized with an audio signal, with an encoding traceable to the film library of Babel).

the image in its entirety: what moves are things in the image. Hence the basic assumption that movies show "pictures of the same thing in different stages of a movement" (Danto 2006: 108). The impression of movement is therefore the combination of a feature of the film ("pictures of the same thing in different stages of a movement") and of a cognitive performance of the spectator, who produces movement out of the successive pictures of the same thing in different stages. It is a synthesis that mobilizes the Kantian categories of substance ("the same thing") and of cause ("in different stages": post hoc ergo propter hoc), with greater relevance than that originally envisioned: in fact, in movies it is undoubtedly the subject that finalizes substantiality and causality (think of the emblematic case of cartoons), while the dependence of real experience from transcendental faculties is more problematic[9].

Such a definition of the "impression of movement", with its decisive objective component ("pictures of the same thing in different stages"), provides an effective tool to find some order in the Film Library of Babel. Indeed, well-formed films would contain sequences of frames with significant degrees of persistence ("images of the same thing...") and of difference ("... in different stages"), while the other elements of the library could be discarded as "audiovisual jumbles"[10]. Here it must be stated first of all that the impression of movement, thus defined, does not necessarily concern the entire film, but only the segments (frames) that compose it, from which follows a complementary property: the possibility of editing, that is, the combination of two segments each with its own impression of movement. Editing is therefore an essential property of the film intended as an object of experience: even in a work composed of a single long shot, in fact, the viewer can legitimately expect a cut at any time, and therefore his experience of the film is always determined at the same time by the impression of movement and the possibility of editing.

Now, there are two borderline cases that have attracted the attention of both Carroll and Danto: on the one hand films composed of still images

---

9   This problematic aspect is analysed in *Goodbye, Kant* (Ferraris 2004: 102-106).
10   The Mpeg video compression algorithms, which are at the basis of the DVD and DivX formats, are based on coding the differences between frames (while not coding the persistences), instead of coding all the frames. A "well-formed" film, in this sense, is a compressible film. This leads to the conceivability, at least at a theoretical level, of a computer program able to clean up the Film Library of Babel. In terms of generative grammars, a minimal representation of a "well-formed film" is as follows: $S \rightarrow sF$ (film beginning); $F \rightarrow fG$ (shot-beginning frame); $G \rightarrow hG$ (shot-continuing frame); $G \rightarrow F$ (cut); $G \rightarrow Ge$ (end of film).

(the proverbial *La jetée* by Marker, but also think of monochromes such as *Blue* by Jarman and *Branca de neve* by Monteiro); on the other, abstract films such as *Mothlight* by Brakhage or McLaren's *Begone Dull Care*. In the first case there would seem to be only invariance (there is "the same thing" but the "different moments" are missing); in the second only difference (there are the "different moments" but the "same thing" is missing). Both these anomalies, however, can be traced back to the idea of a "well formed" film: in the case of mere invariance the difference is assured by sound[11], while in the case of mere difference we can still recognize invariances at the elementary level of lines and colours. However, these concessions risk increasing the margins of uncertainty and subjectivity in the selection of "well-formed" films (to what extent do the variations in sound have to be significant to compensate for the fixedness of the image? To what extent can we call small coloured segments "things"?). On closer inspection, though, there is an even more general problem. In a cultural system where the status of art is given to Duchamp's pissoir, Warhol's Brillo Box and Manzoni's faeces, one cannot exclude that in a suitable context the same could go for a film showing a black silent screen for two hours, or the recording of an interference signal, or the result of a random computer function. If we accept the axiom that "every object can be a work of art" – albeit in a weak, circumscribed and mesoscopic form[12] – then it follows that, when it comes to cinema, anything in the Film Library of Babel can be a film.

---

11 The history of cinema also contemplates the existence of a film entirely made of sound: *Weekend* (1930) by Walter Ruttmann is "a phono-film", without images but only voices, noises and music recorded on optical sound film, using only the audio tape (Bandirali 2004: 30). By the way, in the film library of Babel there are also all the sound recordings of the world, and recorded music is reduced to a subspecies of the film.

12 That is, excluding works of abnormal duration or size, limiting ourselves to "medium-sized" objects, as suggested in *La fidanzata automatica* (Ferraris 2007b: 78-79, 105-111). For Benjamin (1955: 56), the arbitrary transformation of any object into a work of art historically derives from the advent of photography and cinema, which bring things into the artistic domain as they are: if the photograph of a urinal can be an artwork, why should its exhibition not be art as well? The assumption that "anything can be a work of art" has a disputable effect on criticism, generating the specular thesis that "anything can be said of a work of art".

6. *The explanation of the film as a social object*

The Goodmanian distinction between autographic and allographic – in the formulation we have derived from Kivy's ontology – leads to distinguish between works that consist of material objects (the products of autographic arts) and works that consist of ideal objects (the products of allographic arts). After seeing how film has historically evolved from a material object to an ideal object – that is, to an element of the Film Library of Babel – the need has arisen to clean up the chaos of the library using the definition of "moving image", which requires redefining the film as an object of experience.

How is it possible to ensure the unity of the filmic object when its instances are divided into such heterogeneous ontological categories? The most plausible solution seems to require the placement of art in the middle ground between ideality and materiality, in that evolution of the object of experience from the individual field to the collective domain which leads to the realm of social ontology. For Searle (2006: 38) the social object is an entity X which, by virtue of a collective recognition, performs a function Y in a given context C, while in Ferraris's variant social objects are inscribed acts, involving at least two people, recorded on a material surface (even only in the minds of the people involved), which "seem to stand halfway between the materiality of physical objects and the immateriality of ideal objects."(2007a: 67).

The transition to social ontology requires walking down a road that neither Danto nor Carroll have considered: the possibility of regarding the film as an ontologically significant entity regardless of its status as a work of art. If by film we mean the existing counterparts of the "well-formed" elements (based on the impression of movement) of the Film Library of Babel, then the objects that meet the definition are not only the cinematic works presented in the festivals or in arthouse cinemas, but also box office hits, television programs, commercials, CCTV recordings and amateur videos, both those consumed privately and those published on Youtube: all things that in most cases have consciously little to do with the art world. What kind of entity is the film, then? What is its structure? What are its peculiarities?

Let's try to follow the tree scheme of the hierarchical taxonomy of facts on which Searle's (1995) social ontology is based. *At the first level*, it is a matter of choosing between brute physical facts and mind-dependent facts: the film is a mind-dependent fact in the sense that the impression of movement depends on a subjective performance. *At the second level* there is a distinction between intentional and unintentional facts: the film is an intentional fact because the subjective performance is directed towards an object made up of images and sounds. *At the third level*, the choice is between singular and collective facts: the film is a collective fact because intentionality can affect several individuals at the same time (the assertion "viewers are watching a movie" corresponds to Searle's example that "hyenas are hunting a lion"). *On the fourth level,* there is the discrimination between functional facts (where collective intentionality assigns a function to the object) and non-functional facts: the film is a functional fact because it has the primary function of representing movement (secondary purposes aside, viewers watch a film primarily to witness the representation of movement, not to see a series of photographs projected at a twenty-four per second rate). *On the fifth level*, the alternative is between non-agentive functions (inherent in the object) and agentive functions (imposed by the subject): the film is an agentive function because the representation of movement depends on the standard human perceptual apparatus (a creature with a different perception system, for example Funes the memorious, could actually enjoy the film as a succession of distinct images). *On the sixth level*, the agentive function splits into causal functions (determined by the object) and institutional functions (conventionally established by collective intentionality): the film is a "causal function" because the representation of movement depends on the internal configuration of the object, which is not reduced to a conventional feature. So, the film is a social fact in a broad sense, as it is endowed with a collective intentionality and an agentive function, but it is not a social fact in the strict sense (that is, an institutional fact), since its agentive function has a causal nature. The formula "X = series-of-images-and-sounds counts as Y = representation-of-movement in C = context-of-projection" accounts for the presence of film in the domain of social ontology, but places it in a peripheral area that Searle's theory – centered on the paradigm of language and, consequently, on conventionality and on institutionalism – makes it difficult to circumscribe.

In Ferraris's ontology, as said, social objects are defined as recorded acts that involve at least two people. Let's try to apply this definition to the film: the act here consists of the process of realization of the work, in all its possible phases (from the script to staging, from shooting to editing), while the inscription consists of recording this act on a medium (the film, the magnetic tape, or a digital memory). As for the involvement of at least two people, two figures are necessarily involved in filmmaking: the author (the one who performs the act) and the viewer (the one who makes use of, or will be able to make use of, the inscription). A problematic case in this sense could be that of surveillance cameras, which produce apparently authorless recordings (there are neither screenplays, nor staging, nor editing, but only automatically taken shots) with no spectators (most of these shots are not seen, nor will ever be seen, by anyone). Yet even in this case the act can be traced back to the intentionality of at least one author (the one who installed the cameras or had them installed), while the inscription, even when not seen by anyone, implies a potential spectator who may see it if necessary (if a diamond has disappeared from a jewelry store, for example, the police will examine the archived videos)[13].

The conception of the film as an inscribed act that involves at least one author and a potential spectator allows us to explain our object in Aristotelian terms, by giving it an efficient cause (the author), a material cause (recording), a formal cause (the representation of movement) and a final cause (the spectator). But in Ferraris's ontology (2008: 255-259), the inscribed act, however decisive, does not exhaust the structure of the social object, which also includes an Archetype (the model) and an Ectype (the thing in which the Archetype is realized): the inscribed act carries out a decisive mediation between them. In the case of cinema, the Archetype / Inscription / Ectype triad provides the overall description of the film as it has progressively emerged in this paper: the Archetype is the film as an element of the Film Library of Babel; the Inscription is the act that "pulls" the film down from the library inserting it in space and time; the Ectype are the copies that spread and preserve the original inscription, making it available for the collective experience. As Archetype, the film has always existed and will always exist as an ideal object; as Inscription, the film begins to exist as a material object; as Ectype, the film continues to exist as a social object.

---

13   Another problematic case may be that in which the author and the spectator coincide. Consider the following article appeared in "Corriere della sera" (July 24, 2008): "Kinky shots at the supermarket. A pensioner filmed the customers' private parts with a micro-camera on a shopping basket". The pensioner in question is the author of the film and is also the only spectator originally intended to benefit from the inscription. Yet his film was eventually also seen by the officers who seized it: the sociality of the film does not depend only on the use actually made or intended for it, but also on the use that *can* be made of it.

7. *Film structure and functions*

Combining the complementary definitions derived from the social ontologies of Ferraris (film = "Inscription that converts the Archetype into the Ectype") and Searle ("X = screened copy counts as Y = representation-of-movement in C = context-of-screening"), we can finally tackle the main issues that, over time, have animated the theoretical debate on cinema: the dualisms expressed as film / reality, film / narration, film / discourse, film / art.

All these dualisms are due to the attribution of a secondary function to the film as a social object:"Y = representation-of-movement counts as Z in C = context-of-vision". The decisive question to answer will therefore be: what is Z? For some theorists (Bazin, Kracauer, Cavell) Z is reality, for others (Balazs, Metz, Casetti) it is the narration; for some (Bellour, Wilson, Livingston) it is the author's discourse, for others (Bordwell, Carroll, Danto) it is art. In discussing these possible determinations of the Z function, I will refer to the taxonomy of symbolic functions that can be found in Goodman: representation (A refers intentionally to B but does not possess it. For instance, Titian's Venus of Urbino represents Venus, a bed, a dog, a room); exemplification (A refers to B and concretely possesses it: the Venus of Urbino exemplifies red, white, pink, perpendicularity and obliquity); expression (A refers to B and metaphorically possesses it: the Venus of Urbino expresses sensuality and intimacy, but also compositional balance and a delicate lighting).

1) Film/reality

A film is *evidential* if the images and sounds of the Archetype correspond – in whole or in part – to light and sound patterns that can be detected in the space-time where the Inscription takes place. That is to say that these images and sounds refer to what happens in concomitance with the inscribed act, concretely owning its traces: therefore they do not simply represent an event, but exemplify it and document it[14]. The evidential function of the film can be compared – with due caution – to the definition of truth as the *adaequatio* of propositions to things. The transition from analogue to digital complicates (but does not nullify) the veracity of the

---

14 This is a special form of exemplification, since what is exemplified it is not a universal through its occurrence, but a particular (an event) through its visualization.

evidential function, whose verification, however, depended on contextual information already at the dawn of the analogical era[15].

The formula of the evidential film is the following: "Y = representation-of-movement counts as Z = exemplification-of-an-event in C = context-of-vision". The *Zapruder* film documents Kennedy's assassination; the propaganda film *The Triumph of the Will* documents the congress of the National Socialist party held in Nuremberg in 1934; the narrative film *Rome Open City* documents the existence of the places and actors involved in the shooting; the traditional animation film *Snow White and the Seven Dwarfs* only documents the existence of a series of hand drawings; the computerized animation film *Ratatouille* documents very little[16].

2) Film/narration

A film is narrative if the images and sounds of the Ectype are not directly related to the events they bear the trace of, and are instead about a possible world, which may be a version of the real world (historical and biographical films), a plausible variant of it (comedy, drama), or an eccentric reformulation of it (science fiction, fantasy)[17]. The resulting formula of the narrative film

---

15   The recurring scandals about videos released through sites like Youtube, violating the privacy of the filmed person, show that the film continues to play its evidential role even in the digital age: no author of such treacherous videos has ever claimed that the images and sounds were not recorded live but entirely computer-generated. However, in a technologically more advanced society where it is possible to artificially synthesize images and sounds of any kind, it cannot be excluded that the veracity of the evidential function may be drastically weakened (cf. Manovich 2001).

16   This is because an animated film currently still documents the voices of voice actors and the performance of music, and even with computer-generated voices and music it would still exemplify the extension of space (therefore also the presence of colour) and the passage of time.

17   For Peter Kivy, "it seems appropriate to describe contentful works of art, at least those of the more important or elaborate kind, as presenting 'worlds' to inhabit imaginatively" (2002: 256-7). For Noël Carroll, the film gives the spectator the mandate to imagine the narrative world; for example, Buster Keaton provides us with pictures of actors and stagings that we use to imagine what is going on in the world of *The General* (cf. 2006: 184). In recognizing the representation of worlds as a basic function of narrative films, Kivy and especially Carroll emphasize the faculty of imagination. But a film does not only ask us to imagine a world: it represents it in images and sound. While the role of the imagination is central to literature, in cinema it is limited to two secondary aspects: on the one hand, a redirection function – traditionally designated as "suspension of disbelief" – by which we refer the images and sounds perceived to the narrative world rather than the real world; on the other hand, a function of completion, in the sense that we

is: "Y = representation-of-movement counts as Z = representation-of-a-possible-world in C = context-of-vision". In this perspective, the fictional entities are established with a referral structure similar to that with which social objects are created, as can be deduced by comparing the cinematic formula "H = actor counts as K = character in C = narration" with the academic formula "H = person counts as K = professor in C = university"[18]. But there is a decisive difference between the two formulas: the professor also exists in the real world, in the same portion of space-time as the person who has that profession, while the character needs a special space-time which can only be that of a possible world[19].

The distinction between evidential function and narrative function is independent of the form of the Archetype, while it is determined by the contingency of the Inscription. This means that, taking a random element of the Film Library, we are not able to establish whether it is an evidential or a narrative film: in theory it could correspond very well to either function. A science fiction movie could appear for the first time as a representation of a possible world, and then reappear after a few centuries as a reproduction of the real world; a historical film could have the opposite fate. This is a problem that can be traced back to the "paradox of indiscernibles" whose solution is one of the crucial points of Danto's aesthetics: two perceptually identical works can still be differentiated in contextual and relational terms. To determine whether a film is evidential or narrative, it is necessary to know the background of the Inscription, i.e. the context in which the film was produced and consequently the type of reference (to the real world or to the possible world) that its spectators are called to make.

---

must imagine everything that is outside the frame (which also happens in our experience of the real world, of which we have only a partial view that we integrate with the imagination).

18   The establishment of narrative entities through the referral structure is more evident in cinema than in literature: in cinema it is common to distinguish between the documentary genre (where the actor refers to himself as a real person) and the biographical genre (where the actor refers to a character who happens to be a real person), while in literature both genres fall into the non-fiction category.

19   If the heroes of novels and movies existed in the real world, we could meet them on the street; if they did not even exist in a possible world, it would be unexplainable why readers and spectators attribute concrete properties to them and are interested in their fate. Following Kripke's (1980) indication, the term "possible world" should be replaced with "counterfactual world", as the fictitional universe is constructed with reference structures starting from the experience of factual reality and is integrated through a "completion principle" – introduced by Pavel (1986) and specified by Carroll (2006: 181) – by which we *prima facie* assume that the fictional world function like our actual world and imagine consequently.

3) Film/discourse

It has been argued that it is not appropriate to speak of cinematic language, if not in reference to the numerical notation that encodes the recording of films but is alien to the nature of the creative act. The Inscription that transforms the Archetype of the Film Library into the Ectype of the film is therefore not a linguistic act, but is nevertheless an expressive act that involves a series of intentional choices. Instead of language, we can speak of discourse in the sense of the expression of a thought, an idea, a thesis, or more generally in the sense of a line of conduct, of an orientation that affects the act. More precisely, the film's discourse includes everything that in the Ectype can be recognized as determined by an intentionality underlying the act of inscription. The general formula is: "Y = representation-of-movement counts as Z = expression-of-thoughts-and-choices in C = context-of-vision". Each film in this sense has its own discourse: even the positioning of a surveillance camera responds to a strategy and involves the determination of some formal parameters; the difference between a surveillance video and a commercial, or between a pornographic film and an art film, is the quantity, density and expressive importance of these parameters.

In a similar way to the distinction between evidential and narrative, the determination of the discursive function requires leaving the Film Library and considering the film as a social object, that is, as a historically placed Inscription. An element of the Film Library, in fact, can represent both the result of an intentional act and a random process, and in theory could be produced twice, in two different situations, once by chance and the other by intention. Only after having placed the film on the historical horizon in which the Inscription took place, can the spectator wonder about the discourse expressed by the work.

4) Film/art

So far, we have identified three secondary functions of the film: probation (exemplification), narration (representation) and discourse (expression). A film generally combines these three functions in different doses: for example, surveillance videos focus on the evidential function, excluding narration and minimizing expression; cartoons concentrate on the narrative function limiting the discursive component and above all the exemplificative one; special effects use the discursive function to integrate representation and exemplification; avant-garde abstract films reduce exemplification and nullify representation to the benefit of expression.

So, I propose to consider the artistic quality of the film as a tertiary function that depends on the aforementioned secondary functions (evidential exemplification, narrative representation, discursive expression), just as the latter depend on the primary function (representation of movement). Among the secondary functions, the discursive expression identifies a necessary condition for the artisticity of a film (the work of art, to be such, must be attributable to an expressive intentionality), but not a sufficient one (even commercials, for example, express feelings and concepts). The trait that I consider most relevant for the attribution of the artistic status is the relevance of the link between expression on the one hand and exemplification or representation on the other, that is, the possibility of recognizing a supplement of meaning in the dialectic between expressive discourse and worldly appearance (be it exemplificative or representative)[20].

Given the formula "U = link-between-discourse-and-appearance-in-the-film counts as V = work-of art in C = context-that-recognizes-its-relevance", it remains to be established whether dualism is imposed on the context or whether the relevance of dualism is dictated by the context itself. It is a problem similar to the one we encountered at the "sixth level" of Searle's tree, where we were at the crossroads between "causal functions" (determined by the object) and "institutional functions" (conventionally established by collective intentionality). While the representation of movement was clearly a causal function of the filmic object, art is a far more controversial element. Often the choice between causation and conventionality depends on the additional function of meaning assigned to the artistic object: theories that assign to the work of art a function of candidacy for appreciation (Dickie) or social distinction (Bourdieu), tend to embrace conventionality; theories that identify in art an affective function (Ferraris's "automatic sweetheart") or a cognitive function (Goodman's "symptoms of the aesthetic") tend towards causation. Each of these proposals has a peculiar explanatory power: Dickie's institutional theory accounts for experimental videos and found

---

20   This definition of a work of art, centered on the relevance of the link between what appears and what made it appear, can account for the legal distinction between "external form" (worldly appearance) and "internal form" (discursive intentionality) on which copyright is based. For Chatman (1978) the work is marked by the dualism between story and discourse; for Doležel (1998), by the dialectic between a world and its discursive "texture". Lastly, this theoretical position contributes to explaining the two-faced ontology of fictitious entities (see Barbero: 2005), which are both concrete (as capable of worldly appearance) and abstract (as determined by a discursive intentionality).

footage (the cinematic equivalent of ready-mades) while Bourdieu's explains why we can enjoy boring and even unlikable movies; Ferraris's causal theory demonstrates the plausibility of Stendhal's syndrome (even in its reduced form for which viewers cry during a film) while Goodman's points towards a possible solution of the "paradox of horror" (I accept to feel fear watching a horror movie so that I can experience fear). Apparently conventional functions better explain the artistic avant-gardes, while causal functions are more easily applied to the classics and to popular art; however, in most cases, different theories provide different and complementary views on the same object.

This epistemological pluralism confirms the polyhedric and problematic character of the artistic function of cinema, against the linearity of secondary functions (evidential exemplification, narrative representation, discursive expression) and of the primary function (the representation of movement). It is on these basic functions that cinema as art is founded, it is from them that it gradually emerges, and it is within them that in any case it must be placed. Cinematic works are in fact a small province of all films, which in turn make up a tiny region of the Film Library of Babel; similarly, the art world is a small province of social reality, which is itself a tiny region of the universe.

Bibliographical References

Bandirali, L., *Focus on sound:Weekend*, "Segnocinema" n° 130, November 2004

Barbero, C. *Madame Bovary: Something Like a Melody*, Milano, Albo Versorio, 2005

Benjamin, W., *Das Kunstwerk im Zeitalter seiner technischen Reproduzierbarkeit* (1936) in *Schriften*, Frankfurt am Main, Suhrkamp Verlag. English translation available at http://classes.dma.ucla.edu/Winter13/8/WalterBenjaminTheWorkofArt.pdf

Borges, J. L., *Ficciones*, Buenos Aires, Emecé, 1944

Bourdieu, P., *La distinction*, Paris, Les éditions de minuit, 1979

Carroll, N. and Choi, J., ed. by, *Philosophy of Film and Motion Pictures: An Anthology*, Oxford, Blackwell, 2006

Carroll, N., *Defining the Movie Image* (1996), in Carroll and Choi 2006 – *The Philosophy of Motion Pictures*, Oxford, Blackwell, 2008

Chatman, Seymour, *Story and Discourse: narrative structure in fiction and film*, Cornell University Press, Ithaca – London, 1978

Cooper, S., Dann, W. P., Pausch, R., Learning to Program with Alice, New York, Prentice Hall, 2006

Currie, G., The Long Goodbye: The Imaginary Language of Film (1993), in Carroll and Choi 2006

Danto, A. C., Moving Pictures (1979), in Carroll and Choi 2006

Dickie, G., Art and the Aesthetic, Ithaca (N.Y.), Cornell University Press, 1974

Doležel, Lubomír, Heterocosmica. Fiction and Possible Worlds, The John Hopkins University Press, Baltimore-London, 1998

Ferraris, M., Goodbye Kant! Cosa resta oggi della Critica della ragion pura, Milano, Bompiani, 2004

– Sans Papier. Ontologia dell'attualità, Firenze, Castelvecchi, 2007a

– La fidanzata automatica, Milano, Bompiani, 2007b

– Il tunnel delle multe. Ontologia degli oggetti quotidiani, Torino, Einaudi, 2008

Goodman, N., Languages of Art: An Approach to a Theory of Symbols, Indianapolis, The BobbsMerrill, 1968

Jackendoff, R., Lerdahl, F., The generative theory of tonal music, The MIT Press, Cambridge 1983

Kivy, P., Introduction to a Philosophy of Music, Oxford, Clarendon Press, 2002

Kripke, S., Naming and Necessity. Cambridge, Mass.: Harvard University Press (1980)

Livingston, P., Cinematic Authorship (1997), in Carroll and Choi 2006

Manovich, Lev : The Language of New Media, MIT Press, Cambridge Mass, USA, 2001

Pavel, Thomas, Fictional Worlds, Harvard University Press, Cambridge, 1986

Searle, J. R., The Construction of Social Reality, New York, Free Press, 1995

2.
THE DIGITAL SECRET OF THE MOVING IMAGE

1. *Introduction: Ontology and Definition of Cinema*

Cinema, arguably like any other art form, raises two main metaphysical issues. First, an *ontological issue*, concerning the basic ontological category to which a given cinematic work belongs, and second, a *definition issue*, concerning the criteria whereby we can establish whether a given entity is or is not a cinematic work. Addressing the ontological issue for a certain form of art leads us to establish a necessary condition that contributes to addressing the definition of this very form of art. Indeed, if cinematic works belong to a certain ontological category, then a given entity, in order to be a cinematic work, must belong to that same category.

Most authors who have tried to define or characterize cinema have overlooked such an ontological issue. For example, André Bazin argues that cinematic work is a special "mummy," which preserves events instead of bodies[1]. Yet, he does not specify which ontological category such "mummy" should belong to. Likewise, Roman Ingarden characterized the film as "a unique visible music of the transformation of things and of living persons in a spatial world," while Stanley Cavell claimed that the film is "a moving image of skepticism"[2]; yet, neither Ingarden nor Cavell specify what ontological category things like "visible music" or "moving image of skepticism" should belong to.

On the other hand, Walter Benjamin provides us with a useful insight for an ontological characterization of cinema, suggesting that a key feature of cinematic works is their "technical reproducibility"[3]. Still, Benjamin aims

1 André Bazin, "Ontologie de l'image photographique," in *Qu'est-ce que le cinéma?* (Paris: Les Éditions du Cerf, 1958), 14.
2 Roman Ingarden, *Untersuchungen zur Ontologie der Kunst: Musikwerk. Bild. Architektur. Film* (Tübingen: Max Niemeyer, 1962), 338. Stanley Cavell, *The World Viewed* (enlarged edition), (Boston: Harvard University Press, 1979), 188.
3 Walter Benjamin, "Das Kunstwerk im Zeitalter seiner technischen Reproduzierbakeit" in *Schriften* (Frankfurt am Main: Suhrkamp Verlag, 1955).

to highlight social and cultural consequences of technical reproducibility rather than to investigate its ontological underpinnings.

In the history of the attempts to define or characterize cinema, Noël Carroll was, it appears, the first scholar who made the dependence of definition on the ontological issue explicit[4]. Carroll's definition of what he calls "the moving image" includes an insightful ontological account of cinema. But I believe that the connection between ontology and the definition of the moving image requires further investigation.

With this aim in mind, I shall start by introducing the five conditions that constitute Carroll's definition of the moving image. Some of these conditions treat the moving image as a particular display, while others treat it as a type, a non-particular entity that can be instantiated by particulars (§II). The latter conditions raise an ontological puzzle in the case in which the moving image is a digital movie. In this case, the moving image as a type is instantiated by a digital encoding which in turn is a type; therefore, the digital encoding of a digital movie enigmatically ends up in being both a type and a token. Solving such puzzle leads us to conceive of the moving image as *a type that specifies a spatiotemporal distribution of pixels* (§III). I shall argue that this new definition can autonomously take into account all those specifically cinematic features which Carroll accounted for by means of his five conditions (§IV, §V, §VI, §VII, VIII). Finally, I shall investigate the key notions of pixel and type in more depth, thereby establishing to what extent an account of the moving image as a type involves an account of cinema as a Platonic form of art (§IX, §X).

2. *Carroll's Definition of the Moving Image*

Carroll addresses the problem of definition by describing five conditions an entity x must satisfy in order to qualify as a moving image:

1) "x is a detached display"[5]. More specifically, the cinematic display consists of a "visual array," and it is "detached" since it provides the spectator with the visual experience of a space which is not connected to her body[6]. The space S presented by the display does not allow the spectator to orient

---

4   Noël Carroll, *Theorizing the Moving Image* (New York: Cambridge University Press, 1996).

5   Ibid., 70.

6   Ibid., 61.

her body with respect to S through an experienced connection between S and her body. The display provides the spectator with a perspective on a space, but this perspective is reduced to a "disembodied viewpoint"[7]. Through the display, the spectator experiences a space that is not her space.

2) "x belongs to the class of things from which the impression of movement is technically possible"[8]. That is to say, the cinematic display is technically produced in such a way that it can provide the spectator with a visual experience of movement.

3) "Performance tokens of x are generated by a template that is a token"[9]. In claiming that x has tokens, Carroll is presupposing that x is a type, a non-particular entity that can be instantiated by particulars. Furthermore, Carroll calls "templates" those particulars that instantiate x in virtue of their being objects (e.g., film print, videotape, DVD, computer file), while he calls "performance tokens" those particulars that instantiate x in virtue of their being events, namely screenings.

4) "Performance tokens of x are not artworks in their own right"[10]. That is, the screening of a movie, unlike the execution of a symphony or the staging of a play, is not artistically evaluable in its own right. What one can artistically assess is nothing but the movie as a type.

5) "x is [...] two-dimensional"[11]. That is, the visual array constituting the cinematic display is just a flat surface.

In a later text, Carroll strengthens his definition by arguing that the five necessary conditions are also jointly sufficient[12]. In the previous account, Carroll characterized the conditions as necessary but not jointly sufficient, since he did not intend to include among the moving images some artifacts (such as flip books and the zoetrope) that nonetheless satisfy all the necessary conditions. Yet, in the new account, Carroll changes his mind, thereby treating those artifacts as full-fledged moving images. Thus, he turns his necessary conditions into jointly sufficient ones:

---

7   Ibid., 63.
8   Ibid., 70.
9   Ibid.
10   Ibid.
11   Ibid.
12   Noël Carroll, *The Philosophy of Motion Pictures* (Oxford: Blackwell, 2008), 53-79.

So, x is a moving image if and only if (1) x is a detached display or a series thereof; (2) x belongs to the class of things from which the promotion of the impression of movement is technically possible; (3) performance tokens of x are generated by templates that are themselves tokens; (4) performance tokens of x are not artworks in their own right; and (5) x is two-dimensional. Notice that each of these five conditions is alleged to be necessary and to be conjointly sufficient[13].

It is worth noting that conditions (3) and (4) are ontological requirements that establish *what kind of entity* a moving image is, while conditions (1), (2), and (5) rather specify *what further features an entity of that kind* must possess in order to be a moving image. Let us call the former *type-conditions* and the latter *display-conditions*.

Carroll's definition has been criticized both as *too* essentialist by Trevor Ponech and as *not* essentialist *enough* by Thomas Wartenberg. Still, both such criticisms focus mainly on display-conditions rather than on type-conditions. Ponech focuses on condition (1) and argues that the essence of the moving image can be made explicit by revealing the structure of its displays[14]. Wartenberg focuses on condition (5) by arguing that the requirement of two-dimensionality makes the nature of the moving image strongly dependent on our current historical context in which technologies for the production holograms are still not available[15].

Unlike Ponech and Wartenberg, I shall criticize Carroll's definition by focusing on type-conditions and their relationship to display-conditions. For this purpose, I start by questioning whether the term x really refers to the same kind of entity in these two groups of conditions.

On the one hand, in display-conditions, x seems to refer precisely to a display, that is, a two-dimensional visual array that portrays a detached space, and may trigger the impression of movement. On the other hand, in conditions (3) and (4) x designates the moving image as a type having

---

13   Ibid., 73.
14   Trevor Ponech, "The Substance of Cinema," *Journal of Aesthetics and Art Criticism*, 64 (2006), 191: "I agree that such displays are 'detached.' My reasons go a bit beyond Carroll's, though. [...] I identify cinema with the visual display."
15   Thomas Wartenberg, "Carroll on the Moving Image," *Cinema: Journal of Philosophy and the Moving Image*, 1 (2010), 78, http://www4.fcsh.unl. pt:8000/~pkpojs/index.php/cinema/index: "How do we know now that future developments in the moving image will not affect our willingness to call something a moving image in such a way that the necessary conditions Carroll has laid down will be violated?"

templates and performances as its tokens. Yet the display, as a visual array, should be a *particular* entity, whereas the type, as such, is a *non-particular* entity[16]. How can the putative moving image *x* be both particular and non-particular?

Of course, it cannot. Since the type unquestionably is a non-particular, the only way to reconcile the moving image as type with the cinematic display is to conceive of the display as the last step in the instantiation of such type. In other words, the display should not be identified with the moving image as such, but rather with the instance of the moving image that Carroll calls "performance token."

Thus, we can rephrase Carroll's definition by claiming that the moving image is a type that can be instantiated by a display that should be (1) detached; (2) capable of triggering the impression of movement; (3) produced by means of a template; (4) non-artistically-evaluable as such; and (5) two-dimensional. Nevertheless, once we turn to the special case of the *digital* moving image, then Carroll's definition, even in such different guise, raises a puzzle, which I will focus on in the following section.

3. *The Puzzle of the Digital Type*

Carroll claims that the main difference between theatre and cinema is that "the play performance is generated by an interpretation that is a type, whereas the performance of the motion picture is generated by a template that is a token"[17]. Furthermore, in his 1996 book, he claims that the cinematic template "is a film print, but it might also be a videotape, a laser disk, or a *computer program*"[18]. And, in his 2008 book, he specifies that the cinematic template "was a film print, but in recent decades it might be a videotape, a laser disk, a DVD, or an *instantiated computer program*"[19].

I see Carroll's adding of the adjective "instantiated" to the term "computer program" as the clue of a peeping puzzle. If the cinematic template is *a computer program*, as Carroll writes in 1996, then the

---

16   Peter Strawson, *Individuals* (London: Methuen 1959), 231-233. On the one hand, "[p]articulars have their place in the spatio-temporal system, or, if they have no place of their own there, are identified by reference to other particulars which do have such a place." On the other hand, the type is an entity "of which there are many particular instances but which is itself a non-particular."

17   Carroll, *Theorizing the Moving Image*, 70.

18   Carroll, *Theorizing the Moving Image*, 67, my emphasis.

19   Carroll, *The Philosophy of Motion Pictures*, 66, my emphasis.

evidence that a computer program is a *type* which is made of digital symbols contradicts Carroll's aforementioned claim that the cinematic template is a *token*. In his 2008 book, Carroll tries to avoid such contradiction by specifying that, in the digital case, the cinematic template is not a computer program but an *instantiated* computer program. Yet, in the latter case, a new puzzle pops up.

Consider a moving image whose template is an instantiated computer program, or better yet, an instantiated digital file, which consists of traces or circuits. Such a concrete particular is both the template token of a cinematic type C (i.e., the moving image as type) and the token of a digital type D (i.e., the file as sequence of digits). We thus have two types at play. Are those C and D the same type or two different types? In the latter case, what exactly is the relation between C and D?

At a first sight, C and D seem to be completely different types. As pointed out by Nicholas Wolterstorff and Julian Dodd, the cinematic type C specifies what visual qualities ought to be instantiated by showings[20]. By contrast, the digital type D specifies a sequence of digital symbols, so that D is not instantiated by visual showings but rather by physical representations of this sequence of symbols.

Still, C and D are related to one another, since D specifies the sequence of symbols that allows C to be instantiated by a visual array. A token of D, if coupled with an appropriate device capable of translating the digital symbols into chromatic values, behaves as a cinematic template whereby C is instantiated by a showing.

To sum up, the shift from an analog template to a digital template involves a change in the instantiation of the moving image. In the analog case, the whole instantiation required a two-stage process: first, the moving image was embodied by a template; second, the template was used to generate a screening. In the digital case, the structure of instantiation is more complicated. The moving image is not directly embodied by a physical template, but rather encoded by a digital template which is in turn a type, namely, the digital type. The sequence of symbols specified by such digital type is embodied by a physical particular (made of traces or circuits) which is finally used to generate a screening. Therefore, in the digital case,

---

20 Nicholas Wolterstorff, *Works and Worlds of Art* (Oxford: Clarendon, 1980), 94. Julian Dodd, *Works of Music: An Essay in Ontology* (Oxford: Oxford University Press, 2007), 16. According to Wolterstorff, the moving image is a type instantiated by "an occurrence of a sequence of illuminated colour-patterns (counting black and white as colours)." According to Dodd, "a film, after all, is just a type whose tokens are datable, locatable showings."

the whole instantiation of the moving image requires a three-stage process: first, the cinematic type is encoded by a digital type; second, such digital type is embodied by a physical particular; third, such a particular is used to generate a screening.

The mediation of the digital type D between the cinematic type C and its final showing allows us to understand exactly what C itself is. The structure of C, indeed, has to be such that it can be encoded by means of the structure of D. In the digital type D, symbols are placeholders for light values, which correspond to chromatic qualities. I will call such values *pixels*. A pixel, so understood, is not the digital encoding of a light value, but the light value itself.

Furthermore, D is structured in a temporal series of frames, each of which is made of a spatial distribution of pixels. Since the structure of D is aimed to encode the constitutive features of C, should we infer that C consists of a temporal series of frames which are made of spatial distributions of pixels?

Such a question forces us to face the two horns of a dilemma: either a cinematic type C cannot be wholly encoded by a digital type D, or C should have constitutive features that can all be encoded by D. Choosing the first option amounts to claiming that there are movies that cannot be digitally encoded, but this claim seems to contradict our practices concerning movies and their appreciation. For example, the practice of digital restoration of early films would no longer make any sense if old analog films have constitutive features that cannot be encoded by the structure of the digital type[21].

Thus, we are left with the second option. Since the only features that can be encoded by the digital type concern temporal series of frames and spatial distributions of pixels, choosing the second horn of the dilemma amounts to acknowledging that the cinematic type is wholly characterized by temporal series of frames and spatial distributions of pixels. Here is the new definition of cinema. *The moving image is nothing but a type specifying a temporal series of frames that are made of spatial distributions of*

---

21   Scholars like Rodowick or Aumont suggest that analog movies have features that digital movies necessarily lack. I cannot analyze their arguments in this paper, so I limit myself to observing that endorsing such arguments, in the current era in which almost all cinema is becoming digital, amounts to claiming that a relevant portion of the history of cinema is about to disappear. I do not believe so. Digital technology currently guarantees high definition in such a way that it is hard to see how even very fine texture could not be captured by it. See David Rodowick, *The Virtual Life of Film* (Boston: Harvard University Press, 2007). Jacques Aumont, "Que rest-t-il du cinéma?," *Rivista di estetica*, 46 (2011): 17-32.

pixels. In short, the moving image is a type that specifies a spatiotemporal distribution of pixels.

4. *Rethinking the Moving Image*

The digital encoding of a moving image is not a token template, that is, a concrete particular. It is rather an abstract notational structure that reveals the ontological structure of the moving image as a type. With respect to concrete templates like film strips or videotapes, indeed, the digital encoding has an epistemological advantage, that is, it makes the ontological structure of the moving image explicit. In this sense, technology reveals the essence.

The unpacking of Carroll's condition (3), which concerns the cinematic types and its tokens, leads us to a thorough definition of the moving image. But what about the other four conditions of Carroll's definition? How can they be traced back to the ontological structure that is made explicit by the digital type?

As previously pointed out, conditions (1), (2) and (5) are display-conditions in which x refers to the display that instantiate the moving image, whereas conditions (3) and (4) are type-conditions in which x refers to the moving image as a type that can be instantiated by displays. Addressing the puzzle of the digital type has led us to develop condition (3) so as to define the moving image as a type that specifies a spatiotemporal distribution of pixels, which can be instantiated by displays.

Still, according to Carroll's other conditions, the display that instantiates the moving image has further necessary features; (1) it is detached; (2) it is capable of producing the impression of movement; (4) it is not artistically evaluable; (5) it is two-dimensional. In the following sections I shall argue that all these features of the display can be taken into account in terms of the cinematic type introduced in condition (3). More specifically, I shall consider detachment in section §V, impression of movement in section §VI, two-dimensionality in section §VII, and non-evaluability in section §VIII.

5. *Detachment*

Condition (1) of Carroll's definition states that the cinematic display is detached, that is, in watching the display, the spectator experiences things that are not localizable in the spatiotemporal system that has her body as its center. In other words, the moving image supports an experience that allows the spectator to recognize *what* there is, but not *where* she is with regard to what there is.

Indeed, a particular showing of a moving image is not necessarily detached. I can use my web-cam as a mirror while shaving. In this case I can recognized where I am with regard to the displayed scene. The display is necessarily detached only if it is considered as a token of the moving image as a type. Treating the display as a token requires that the scene displayed be able to be shown in a multiplicity of different spaces, without any special connection to the spectators who inhabit those spaces. If we conceive of the display as a token, then it does not matter whether I can shave by looking at my web-cam. From this perspective, the current display of my web-cam is just the token of a type that can be displayed in a multiplicity of other circumstances. What matters is that the generic spectator of a showing of the moving image produced by my web-cam cannot shave by looking at it. In this sense the cinematic display is detached in virtue of its being the token of a type.

Since the repeatability of the moving image as a type allows this image to be replicated in several different spaces, the displayed space cannot have any special connection to the bodies placed in all those spaces. Repeatability necessarily breaks the spatial connection between the displayed space and the space of the audience. If we consider the display as a particular event, nothing prevents the displayed space from being connected to the space that the beholder inhabits. What makes the displayed space necessarily detached is the repeatability of the moving image as a type. The only token that is connected to the spectator's own space is arguably the particular display that instantiates the moving image during its production, as in the case of a web-cam used as a mirror. But if the display is considered as any token of an existing moving image, then it is necessarily detached from the space of the spectator.

From this perspective, all the "prosthetic devices"[22] (e. g. mirrors, microscopes, telescopes) that Carroll attempts to distinguish from the moving image by means of the detached display condition can be distinguished much more simply by considering that they do not have a type-token ontological structure. Mirrors, as well as other glass-based prosthetic devices, cannot be repeated. They are nothing but visible particulars. They are not tokens of types that specify visual features. There is no type of which several mirrors, being displays, are all tokens. Any mirror displays only its own space. The basic ontological difference between mirrors and

---

22   Carroll, *Theorizing the Moving Image*, 57.

moving images is that the former are just particulars whereas the latter are tokens of types. The fact that moving images are detached display whereas mirrors are not simply follows from such difference.

6. *Impression of Movement*

In formulating condition (2), Carroll considers the spectator's disposition to believe that what the display presents might move, instead of giving the mere impression of movement, because he wants to take into account works such as Marker's *La jetée*, Frampton's *Poetic Justice* and Snow's *One Second in Montreal*, made, partly or wholly, by still images. According to Carroll, these works are different from a mere slide show because spectators of the former can legitimately expect (at least at the first viewing) that sooner or later there will be some movement in the pictures. As Carroll puts is, "it is always justifiable to entertain the possibility that the image *might* move"[23].

I also argue that this condition can derive from the structure of the cinematic type that the digital encoding makes explicit. "To entertain the possibility that the image *might* move" is indeed "always justifiable" because the moving image as a type consists of a series of frames whose temporal rate is capable of affording the impression of movement to our perceptual system. The epistemological possibility (we know that there could be movement) is based upon an ontological possibility (the type consists of a series of frames, so it is capable of affording the impression of movement to us). Paintings and photographs can not move since they consist of a *spatial* distribution of coloured points, whereas the moving image can move (and spectators believe it can) since it consists of a *spatiotemporal* distribution of coloured points.

In short, the movie's content can move since the movie not only occupies a surface, but also has a duration. The moving image does not consist of a series of frames because it can move: it can move because it consists of a series of frames. That is why "movement is a permanent possibility in cinema"[24]. Even in the cases in which the moving image *does not really move*, it *might move*, because the cinematic type carries this possibility in its structure.

---

23   Carroll, *The Philosophy of Motion Pictures*, 60.
24   Ibid., 60.

From this perspective, sound can also be treated as a permanent possibility in cinema, for the same reason as movement. Both sound and movement unfold in time. Therefore, in order to have auditory features, a work must unfold in time. Since the moving image, as a spatiotemporal distribution of pixels, takes place in time, it carries the possibility of sound in its own structure. As the moving image can afford the impression of movement to spectators, so this image can afford the impression that some sound is synchronized with (or, at least, somehow connected to) what is displayed. From this perspective, silent films such as Kaurismäki's *Juha* or Hazanavicius' *The Artist*, which lack *sound* because of stylistic choices (instead of technical limitations), function similarly to "static films"[25] such as Marker's *La jetée* or Godard and Gorin's *Letter to Jane*, which lack *movement* because of stylistic choices. In this sense, the unexpected movement of an eye in a scene of *La jetée* exploits the spectator's attitude to entertain the possibility that the image *might move* even in a static film, as well as the unexpected sound of a glass in a scene of *The Artist* exploits the spectator's attitude to entertain the possibility that the image *might sound* even in a silent film.

Still, if the moving image ultimately is a spatiotemporal distribution of pixels, how can we distinguish moving images from slide shows? Slide shows are also constituted by series of frames, that is, spatiotemporal distributions of pixels. How do they differ from moving images? I argue that slide shows belong to an ontological category that is in between still images and moving images. More specifically, the slide show provides us with an experience that is akin to the experience of still images, but rests upon an ontological structure that is akin to the structure of moving images.

The difference between the slide show and the moving image is basically a matter of frame rate. Below a certain threshold rate R1, the series of frames is experienced as a series of still images. Above a certain threshold rate R2, the series of frames is experienced as a moving image (likewise, a series of musical notes can be heard as a continuous melody only if such notes are played at a rate that is above a certain threshold). In between R1 and R2, the series of frame is experienced as a jerky image, that is, an image that is no longer still but not yet moving.

In spite of lacking the possibility of the impression of movement, slide shows exhibit a distinctive temporal mood. Like moving images, and unlike mere books of images, slide shows can be synchronized with sounds. Yet, the frame rate of a slide show, unlike that of a moving image,

---

25   Ibid., 61.

is not necessarily established by the maker or by the practice, but can be up to the presenter[26].

To sum up, Carroll's conditions (1) and (2), which describe the relation between the cinematic display and the experience of the spectator, can be explained in terms of structural features of the moving image as a type. Cinematic displays afford detachment and impression of movement to the spectator because they are tokens of the moving image, which is a type constituted by a series of frames made of pixels. Detachment and impression of movement are phenomenal and epistemic consequences of the ontological structure of the cinematic type, as well as being transparent and drinkable are phenomenal and epistemic consequences of the chemical structure of water.

7. Two-dimensionality

Carroll introduces the requirement of two-dimensionality in order to exclude "moving sculptures of the sort that are exemplified by the moving figurines on various antique clocks" from the domain of the moving image[27]. This sort of moving sculpture is akin to the moving image to the extent that they both present a detached space in which we can see movement. Furthermore, they have both multiple instances that are produced from a template.

Still, moving sculptures are three dimensional whereas moving images are two-dimensional[28]. The requirement of two-dimensionality is thus sufficient to exclude moving sculptures from the cinematic domain. On the other hand, Carroll acknowledges that this requirement is not sufficient to cleave the moving image from theatre. That is because "there is, in fact, theatre that is two-dimensional, for example the shadow-puppet shows of Bali, Java, and China"[29].

---

26 A quite impressive example of a slide show whose frame rate is up to the performer can be found in the so-called "Kodak Carousel scene" of the TV series *Mad Men* (Season 1, episode 13; the scene is available on YouTube with the title "Mad Men – The Carousel").

27 Ibid., 72.

28 By claiming that moving images are two-dimensional, Carroll means that their screenings take place onto flat surfaces. Of course, what is seen by spectators in such two-dimensional surfaces can (and usually does) consist of three-dimensional scenes.

29 Ibid., 73.

In order to cleave motion pictures from shadow-puppet shows, Carroll exploits his condition (3), namely the type-template-performance condition. But his solution raises a question that he does not explicitly consider. What about a shadow-puppet show made by means of a moving sculpture? Since this sort of shadow-puppet show satisfies both the two-dimensionality requirement and the type requirement, we should conclude – against our intuitions – that it *is* a moving image. Thus, the case of the moving sculpture has not really been explained away by the two-dimensionality condition. If we use moving sculptures in a shadow-puppet show, the problem pops up again.

A supporter of Carroll's definition might by replying such a manufactured shadow-puppet show *is* in fact a moving image since it satisfies all Carroll's conditions. Indeed, Carroll himself seems to invoke a similar argument in his 2008 book, when he claims that manufactured flip books *are* moving images, whereas handmade flip books *are not*[30].

I think that this is an *ad hoc* reply, and a quite unsound one. Indeed, we normally conceive of both handmade images like paintings and manufactured images like photographs or prints as *still images*. Why should we behave differently in the case of *moving images*? Why the handmade/ manufactured divide, which is not relevant in order to establish whether something is or is not a still image, should become relevant when we establish which shadow-puppet shows (or flip books) are moving images and which are not? I see no reason to treat manufactured shadow-puppet shows (or manufactured flip books) as moving images while treating handmade shadow-puppet shows (or handmade flip books) as images of a different kind. The only reason I can see is the defense of Carroll's definition of the moving image.

If you want to include shadow-puppet shows and flip books in the domain of the moving image, you should include *all* shadow-puppet shows and *all* flip books in this domain. Thus, by accepting that manufactured shadow-puppet shows are moving images, Carroll would put his definition on a slippery slope leading to the conclusion that *all* shadow-puppet shows are moving images. In this way, Carroll's definition would be reduced to a variant of Berys Gaut's account, according to which any object-generated image that exhibits movement counts as a moving image, so that even "Plato's parable of the cave in the Republic would also count as a kind of object-generated cinema"[31]. Yet Gaut's account of cinema raises

---

30   Ibid., 75.
31   Cf. Berys Gaut, *A Philosophy of Cinematic Art* (Cambridge: Cambridge University Press, 2010), 6.

two problems that, I argue, are much more puzzling than the problem of manufactured shadow-puppet shows raised by Carroll's definition.

First, if you want to preserve the intuition according to which "still movies" like *Letter to Jane* are moving images, then you should accept any object-generated image that *might* exhibit movement into the domain of the moving image. Such a domain, which in Gaut's account is already immense, is further extended. Even the shadow on the wall that is generated by my table is a moving image, since my table might move, and therefore its shadow *might* move.

Second, in spite of our shared understandings, in Gaut's account cinema is no longer something that has been invented towards the end of the 19th century, but rather something almost as old as the wheel or the knife. From such a perspective, to treat the Lumière Brothers as the inventors of cinema would be as wrong as to treat Gutemberg as the inventor of writing. Indeed, I agree that it is arguable whether the Lumière Brothers really invented cinema. In cinema museums, you can find many screening devices made in the 19th century that somehow anticipate the Lumières' *Cinématographe*. Yet I do not know of any cinema museum in which shadows of tables are exhibited as examples of cinema. In this sense, Gaut's ontology of cinema is too hospitable, even up to the point of contradicting established practices, intuitions, and judgments concerning cinema.

If you want to avoid such a slippery slope towards too hospitable an ontology of cinema, you should find a safer way than Carroll's to prevent moving sculptures from counting as moving images. For this purpose, it is worth setting Carroll's condition (5) (i.e. the two-dimensionality requirement) aside, and looking once again to his condition (3), that is, to the structure of the moving image as a type. Moving sculptures differ from motion pictures because they have different structures at the type level. The type of the moving sculpture is not made of a spatiotemporal distribution of visual qualities, but it rather includes properties such as height, weight, and chemical composition. The moving sculpture is excluded from the cinematic domain because of the different ontological structure of its type, and not because of its three-dimensionality.

Such difference in the ontological structure also explains why the moving image, which is just made of visual (and possibly auditory) qualities, provides us with the *impression of movement* whereas the moving sculpture, which has further physical and chemical features, provides us with *true movement*. Furthermore, the distinctive ontological structure of the moving image as a type allows us to take into account the possibility of holography, whose affinity with the moving image is suggested by

Carroll himself: "Imagine that we could project a scene of mortal combat in the Coliseum three-dimensionally with the audience seated around the virtual arena like ancient Romans. Would not such a spectacle be rightfully categorized as a moving image"[32]?

We need a criterion to distinguish holographic screenings, which our intuition is prone to consider as moving images, from moving sculptures, which we aim to exclude from the cinematic domain. The two-dimensionality condition fails to support this distinction, since Carroll is forced to exclude both moving sculpture and holography from the cinematic domain. But if we pose as a criterion the ontological structure of the type, then we can treat holograms as peculiar cinematic types whose frames are *three-dimensional* distributions of pixels, instead of two-dimensional ones like in ordinary movies. In this way, we can substantially exclude from the cinematic domain only the moving sculptures, whose types are not spatiotemporal distributions of pixels at all, while preserving the cinematic nature of holograms in spite of their three-dimensionality. In short, the ontological structures of types explains why the hologram is not different from the moving image as the moving sculpture is[33].

8. Non-evaluability

Carroll's condition (4) claims that cinematic tokens lack artistic value. I argue that such lack follows from the fact that all you need in order to instantiate a moving image is already specified by the corresponding type, and no further contributions are required. You only need to instantiate the visual (and auditory) patterns constituting a moving image as a type, that is, the patterns established by the makers of the image. Such instantiation can be done with merely automatic processes, in which there is no room for human intentionality and creativity, and, *a fortiori*, for artistic value. By virtue of the cinematic type's ontological structure, once the makers of a moving image constitute it as a type, the subsequent displays will be just a matter of automatic technical processes.

On the other hand, theatrical performance is an interpretation that involves intentional acts. The reason for the sharp difference between

---

32 Carroll, *The Philosophy of Motion Pictures*, 73.
33 Shadow-puppet shows of any kind also differ substantially from moving images since the former are not individuated by discrete spatiotemporal distributions of frames and pixels but rather by continuous spatiotemporal distributions of light and darkness.

cinema and theatre lies precisely in the structure of the type. The theatrical work as a type is just a written text, so in principle it cannot specify all the perceptible properties that should constitute an experienceable instance of the work. In order to turn such a text into a theatrical production you need some creative act of interpretation. By contrast, the cinematic type, as a spatiotemporal distribution of visual qualities, specifies all the relevant experienceable features that constitute an instance of the moving image, leaving no room for interpretation and preventing the screening of a moving image, unlike the presentation of a theatrical performance, from being evaluated as a work of art in its own right.

The structure of the cinematic type, conceived as a spatiotemporal distribution of pixels, is such that, at the token level, it only remains to make those distributions accessible to the viewers. Of course, we can distinguish between better or worse screenings. But such normative distinction only concerns technical procedures. Some displays may correctly instantiate the visual pattern specified by the type (as in the case of high definition copies and high quality projectors), while others may have poor quality (as in the case of VHS copies or old and worn projectors). But the difference between a good and a bad screening of a moving image is not a matter of interpretation at all, let alone of artistic value. It is only a matter of technical approximation to the visual appearance wholly specified by the moving image as a type.

9. Pixels

So far, I have argued that the moving image is *a type specifying a spatiotemporal distribution of pixels*. In these final sections, I shall focus on the fact that not only digital movies but moving images in general are types specifying spatiotemporal distributions of pixels. For this purpose, I shall analyze in more depth the key notions of pixel and type.

According to Ponech, pixels are particular points of light:

> 'Pixel' usually denotes 'picture element.' I use it in a slightly adjusted but related technical sense. By 'pixels' I intend points of light. This usage converges with descriptions of movie images as constructed from separate regions varying independently in spectral distribution. At a basic level of physical description, visual displays are composed of pixels.[34]

---

34   Ponech, "The Substance of Cinema," 191-92.

Pixels, so understood, are constitutive elements of both digital and analog displays. The only difference is that the points of lights constituting a digital display are arrayed in a grid whereas in analog displays they are not. In the latter case, indeed, the spatial distribution of pixels matches the irregular – but nevertheless discrete – distribution of individual grains on the film strip.

The cinematic display is essentially *discrete*, that is, consisting of particular points of lights separated by temporal and spatial interstices. Discreteness is sharply exhibited by the digital display, whose pixels are regularly distributed in a grid. Discreteness also characterizes analog displays, whose pixels are separated by spatial interstices in spite of the lack of a regular grid, since every frame consists of individual grains of colour. Furthermore, both analog and digital pixels belong to frames that are separated from each other by temporal interstices, since analog and digital projectors both show a limited number of frames per second, and since the film of analog projectors alternately blocks and reveals light.

The limit of Ponech's account is the conception of the pixel as a *particular* point of light. The pixel, so understood, can only concern a *particular* display, that is, a *particular* showing of a moving image. It follows that any new showing involves a completely *new* series of pixels on the screen. Therefore, Ponech's characterization of the moving image in terms of pixels cannot take into account the moving image as a repeatable work that can be instantiated by a multiplicity of showings. If the moving image is made of pixels that are no more than particulars, then there is no way to appropriately relate the screening of *Behind the Candelabra* that I watched in London to another screening of the *same* movie that took place in Los Angeles. Therefore, I agree with Ponech that pixels are "the substance of cinema"[35], but I argue that in order to take repeatability of cinematic works into account we should conceive of the pixel not as *a particular point of light*, but rather as *a value of light* which can be instantiated by a multiplicity of particular points of light.

If all of this is right, both digital and analog moving images are types that specify pixels. The only difference is in the way in which the cinematic type specifies the pixels that should be instantiated by displays. In the analog case, pixels are implicitly specified by means of concrete templates, as for example reels of celluloid that allow us to instantiate roughly the same spatiotemporal distribution of light values at each showing of a given moving image. By contrast, in the digital case pixels can be explicitly

---

35   Ibid., 187.

specified as light values, because the template is no longer a concrete object but a series of numbers denoting light values.

In a similar vein, Gaut accounts for digital cinema by conceiving of the pixel as a discrete unit that measures "the light intensity [...] as a discrete integer"[36]. Yet he challenges the claim that, in digital pictures, the pixel is a "minimal denotative unit" by claiming that "the parts of a pixel denote the parts of the area of the object that the pixel denotes [...] The denotation relation still holds at the sub-pixel level. The parts of a pixel do denote, unlike the parts of a word"[37]. That is to say, if we look closely at a pixel on the screen, then we can see a small coloured area whose coloured parts in their turn denote.

I argue that Gaut's argument is wrong, since what we truly see in looking closely at the screen is not the pixel itself, but the particular spot of light that instantiates the light value constituting the pixel. This spot of light is seen as a small coloured area having coloured parts, but the pixel instantiated by this token is a light value having no parts at all. By claiming that in digital pictures the pixel is not a minimal denotative unit, Gaut seems to mistake the ontological nature of the pixel with the empirical fact that the particular spots of light instantiating pixels are not usually recognized by viewers as minimal denotative units. But, in digital pictures, the pixel *is* a *minimal denotative unit* since it is not a particular spot of light but rather a light value that *denotes* the light intensity in a precise spatiotemporal location.

In challenging the claim that in digital pictures the pixel is a minimal unit, Gaut also argues that:

> The digital photograph is not [...] different from a traditional photograph. For the latter is comprised of sometimes billions of individual grains [...] In this respect there is also an array of picture elements in the traditional photograph, albeit one with vastly more elements than is usual in digital photographs, and which are not arrayed in a grid. Keep on enlarging such a photograph, and in the end one will see individual grains, from which the object is not recognizable, even though the grains denote parts of the object.[38]

Still, those considerations do not necessarily show that pixels are not minimal denotative units. Rather, they seem to show that also traditional photographic pictures have minimal denotative units, namely grains, which

---

36   Gaut, *A Philosophy of Cinematic Art*, 57.
37   Ibid., 58.
38   Ibid., 59.

play the role of pixels, in spite of the lack of a notation capable of representing them. Let us consider, in this sense, the example proposed by Gaut:

> This is the lesson of Michelangelo Antonioni's *Blow-Up* (1966): as Thomas, the photographer played by David Hemmings, keeps enlarging the image that he thinks shows a murder, the grains of film become more prominent and it becomes impossible in the end to tell what they denote[39].

If, as Gaut writes, "the grain become more prominent," then the grain has not to be identified with the area it occupies on the paper (or on the screen, if we move from the photographic example to a hypothetical cinematic counterpart of it). An area that becomes *more prominent* is no longer the same area. The grain has rather to be identified with a light value, which could be instantiated by *more or less prominent* areas on the paper (or on the screen). Moreover, in developing the *Blow-Up* case, Gaut claims that, after enlarging the image, "it becomes impossible in the end to tell what [the grains] denote." Yet, in so doing, Gaut conflates two issues: what a grain denotes, and what the picture depicts. Indeed, after enlarging the image, it becomes impossible in the end to tell what the picture depicts, but not what the grains denote. Even enlarged, a grain of a photograph still denotes the light intensity in a precise spatiotemporal location, and that is why the *Blow-Up* photographer keeps on analyzing this photograph with the purpose of understanding what the picture depicts. Grains in analog pictures have to be ultimately identified with light values, or pixels, whereby these pictures depict their subjects.

10. *Types*

In sections from §III to §VIII I have argued that the moving image is *a type* specifying a spatiotemporal distribution of *pixels*. In section §IX I have investigated what a pixel is. In order to seal this definition of the moving image, it only remains to investigate what a type is.

Following Wolterstorff and Dodd, I argue that the moving image is a *normative* type, that is, a type that establishes what visual features a *correct* instance of such image *ought to* exhibit[40]. As normative types, moving images can have two sorts of instances; *incorrect* ones (which only possess some relevant subset of the normative features), and *correct* ones (which

---

39   Ibid., 59.
40   Wolterstorff, *Works and Worlds of Art*, 94. Dodd, *Works of Music*, 16.

possess all the normative features). Conceiving of the moving image as a normative type allows us to take into account an indispensable aspect of our cultural practices, that is, the fact that we usually assess not only cinematic works ("this is a good movie, that is a bad one...") but also instantiations of these works ("this is a faithful screening, that is a flawed one."). Carroll's condition (4) points out that the former is an artistic assessment whereas the latter is rather a technical assessment. Still, they both are assessments, which rest upon some form of normativity. More specifically, the artistic assessment rests upon some standard of taste, whereas the technical assessment rest upon the work itself, understood as a normative type that establishes the standard for its correct screenings.

According to Wolterstorff and Dodd, treating a type as normative obliges us to treat this type as a Platonic universal. Therefore, movies or symphonies, as *normative* types, are "abstract, fixed, unchanging, and eternally existent entities"[41]. Yet, David Davies challenges the claim that conceiving of moving images as normative types commit us to such a counterintuitive Platonic view, according to which movies are not created but discovered[42]. He argues that we can conceive of the moving image as a normative type by considering the Wittgensteinian account of normativity developed by Robert Brandom: "a *pragmatist* conception of norms – a notion of primitive correctnesses of performance *implicit* in *practice* that precede and are presupposed by their *explicit* formulation in *rules* and *principles*"[43].

In such an account of normative types, what establishes whether a particular display D is a correct instance, a flawed instance or a non-instance of a given cinematic work W is not an explicit list of light values residing in the abstract space of the universals where they are grasped and made normative by the filmmaker. Instead, the status of D as an instance of W depends upon an implicit negotiation between two parties: what the filmmaker specifies in making his or her work W public in a given cultural context, and the practices that implicitly establish which displays are fully qualified to play the experiential role in the appreciation of W. According to Davies, there are no explicit rules of correctness for the instantiation of a given moving image W. Practices sanction conditions of appreciation of

41   Dodd, *Works of Music*, 36.
42   David Davies, "What Type of 'Type' is a Film?," in *Art and Abstract Objects*, ed. C. Mag Uidhir (Oxford: Oxford University Press, 2013), 263-83.
43   Robert Brandom, *Making it Explicit: Reasoning, Representing, and Discursive Commitment* (Cambridge: Harvard University Press, 1994), 21.

W, and cinematic displays are technically assessed with respect to the role they play in appreciation of W, but nothing more.

I agree with Davies that normativity of the moving image as a type rests upon cultural practices rather than upon some abstract, fixed, unchanging, and eternally existent entity. Yet, I think that, in this respect, the case of digital cinema requires special treatment, since digital technology allows us to produce instances of a given image (regardless of its being static or moving) that are all "phenomenally identical in respect of colour, shape, and size"[44]. That is because digital technology provides us with a sort of notation whereby we can represent an image W by means of a *script* S of discrete symbols which denote the points of light constituting W. Thus, in order to instantiate W, we only need some device capable of translating the discrete symbols constituting S into the points of light constituting W. If these devices are properly functioning, then all instances of W produced by coupling such devices with S are phenomenally identical.

In principle, digital cinema enables the filmmaker to establish once and for all the only way in which correct instances of her work should appear. Specifying a moving image W by means of a digital script, indeed, amounts to unequivocally establishing the appearance of any correct instance of W. In this way, the standard of correctness for the instances of W is no longer implicit in practice but made explicit by means of the digital script. As a thought experiment, we can even conceive of special digital devices (perhaps embedded in mobile phones) with which moviegoers can check whether the movie they are watching is shown correctly. Such devices could measure light values on the screen and compare them with the original light values approved by the filmmaker and stored in some online database.

If all of this is right, should we conclude that digital technology turns moving images into everlasting Platonic entities? I do not think so. Digital technology is something that was created in the context of our cultural practices. For this reason, what a moving image becomes thanks to digital technology still rests upon our practices.

Nevertheless, digital technology seems capable of supporting what we could call a *Platonic practice*, that is, a way of univocally establishing the appearance of a work that no longer depends on metaphysical virtues,

---

44   John Zeimbekis, "Digital Pictures, Sampling, and Vagueness: The Ontology of Digital Pictures," *Journal of Aesthetics and Art Criticism*, 70 (2012), 51. It is worth noting that, according to Zeimbekis, the digital encoding of pictures is a notational schema but it is not a full-fledged Goodmanian notational system since it lacks Goodman's semantic requirement of finite differentiation.

but rather on technical devices. Such devices are a necessary condition for the rise of a Platonic practice, but not a sufficient one. Agreement is also required. Therefore, cinema can become a Platonic practice, namely *Platonic cinema*, only if practitioners agree that all correct screenings of a moving image W ought to be phenomenally identical by complying with the pixels specified once and for all by the maker of W.

Currently, we have a technique allowing for Platonic cinema, but we do not yet have a practice establishing Platonic cinema as the cinematic medium in force. In spite of the fact that digital technology enables us to make moving images explicit in terms of unique series of pixels, we keep relying on the implicit normativity of cultural practices in order to constitute movies as spatiotemporal distributions of light values. Yet, if we want to be sure of transmitting not just instances but *correct instances* of our movies to future generations, then Platonic cinema, which our technology already enables in principle, is the right way forward.

Bibliographical References

Aumont, Jacques. "Que rest-t-il du cinéma?" *Rivista di estetica*, 46 (2011): 17-32.

Bazin, André. "Ontologie de l'image photographique," in *Qu'est-ce que le cinéma?* Paris: Les Éditions du Cerf, 1958. English translation: "The Ontology of the Photographic Image." *Film Quarterly* 13, 4 (1960): 4-9.

Benjamin, Walter. "Das Kunstwerk im Zeitalter seiner technischen Reproduzierbakeit" in *Schriften*. Frankfurt am Main: Suhrkamp Verlag, 1955. English translation in *The Work of Art in the Age of its Technological Reproducibility, and Other Writings on Media*. Boston: Harvard University Press, 2008.

Brandom, Robert. *Making it Explicit: Reasoning, Representing, and Discursive Commitment*. Cambridge: Harvard University Press, 1994.

Carroll, Noël. *Theorizing the Moving Image*. New York: Cambridge University Press, 1996.

Carroll, Noël. *The Philosophy of Motion Pictures*. Oxford: Blackwell, 2008.

Cavell, Stanley. *The World Viewed* (enlarged edition). Boston: Harvard University Press, 1979.

Davies, David. "What type of 'type' is a film?" In *Art and Abstract Objects*, edited by Christy Mag Uidhir, 263-83, Oxford: Oxford University Press, 2013.

Dodd, Julian. *Works of Music: An Essay in Ontology*. Oxford: Oxford University Press, 2007.

Gaut, Berys. *A Philosophy of Cinematic Art*. Cambridge: Cambridge University Press, 2010.

Ingarden, Roman. *Untersuchungen zur Ontologie der Kunst: Musikwerk. Bild. Architektur. Film*. Tübingen: Max Niemeyer, 1962. English translation: *The Ontology of the Work of Art*. Athens: Ohio University Press, 1989.

Ponech, Trevor. "The Substance of Cinema." *The Journal of Aesthetics and Art Criticism*, 64 (2006): 187-98.

Rodowick, David. *The Virtual Life of Film*. Boston: Harvard University Press, 2007.

Strawson, Peter. *Individuals*. London. Methuen 1959.

Wartenberg, Thomas. "Carroll on the Moving Image." *Cinema: Journal of Philosophy and the Moving Image*, 1 (2010): 69-80, http://www4.fcsh.unl.pt:8000/~pkpojs/index.php/cinema/index.

Wolterstorff, Nicholas. *Works and Worlds of Art*. Oxford: Clarendon, 1980.

Zeimbekis, John. "Digital Pictures, Sampling, and Vagueness: The Ontology of Digital Pictures." *Journal of Aesthetics and Art Criticism*, 70 (2012): 43-53.

MOBILE PHONES

1.
DOUBLE SIGNATURE
An Ontology of the Mobile Movie

If ontology in general is the study of being, the ontology of x is the study of the being of x, that is, the attempt to answer the question: what is x? What kind of object is it? What categories does it fall into? In what horizon is it located? The object x we are dealing with here is the mobile movie, or the film shot with a mobile phone. These linguistically composite expressions – mobile movie, film shot with a mobile phone – refer to an ontologically composite object: an x that derives from the encounter of an object y (the mobile phone) and an object z (the film). We will then start from a preliminary clarification of the ontology of the mobile phone and the ontology of the film, and then try to understand the specific being of the mobile movie, assessing the relevance of this specificity.

1. Ontology of the mobile phone

The mobile phone belongs to the genus of telephone devices, which by definition and etymology make it possible for individuals who are in different places to talk each other. But what traits make the mobile phone special, distinguishing it from other devices of the same kind (for example, a landline telephone, a public telephone, or a cordless phone)? What exactly does "mobility" refer to in the English term mobile phone? And is this characteristic enough to identify the mobile phone or is there something else?

The specific mobility of the mobile phone can be clarified by resorting, with a little ruthlessness, to the Heideggerian lexicon of *Being and Time* (see Ferraris 2005, pp. 47-49). In particular, there are three main features of the mobile phone: 1) *Jemeinigkeit*, the fact that it is my own, individual, customized, as opposed to a landline which can be used by many people; 2) *Zuhandenheit*, the fact that it is ready at hand, it fits in my hand or pocket and therefore can be handled almost anytime, in any situation; 3)

Befindlichkeit, the fact that it is emotionally situated, it is able to involve the affective dimension and arouse the emotional participation of those who use it. So the mobility of the phone induces a transformation of presence, of our being-there (*Dasein*), of our being-in-the-world (*In-der-Welt-sein*). The mobile phone – almost as much as my own body – is exclusively mine (*Jemeinigkeit*); is always with me, ready at hand (*Zuhandenheit*); and involves me emotionally (*Befindlichkeit*).

These factors of transformation of presence help to identify the specificity of the mobile phone but do not exhaust its ontological novelty, which must be integrated using other categories: writing, recording, construction of social reality. Unlike the traditional telephone, the mobile phone is not only used to speak, but is also a typewriter, producing texts of various kinds (text messages, emails, web pages). This writing function is not limited to communication (I send you a text saying "I'll be there at 11" instead of calling you and saying "I'll be there at 11") but mainly consists in recording, that is, in saving empirical data from contingency, ensuring their iterability (because I sent you a text message instead of calling you, we have an external proof of our appointment at 11am). If we then recognize that communicating basically means recording our expressions in the minds of others, then communication itself is reduced to a peculiar case of recording. In this perspective, in fact, I use my mobile phone to write not only when I write (recording in the electronic memory of the device) but also when I speak (recording in the biological memory of the interlocutor). So the phone is not just a "Heideggerian machine", a prosthesis of our presence in the world that reifies and accentuates its features of exclusivity, accessibility and emotional involvement: it is also a "Derridean machine", a prosthesis of memory that predisposes us to write and record, that is, to defer being to the trace, in any situation.

Provided that the specificity of the mobile phone is identified by the transformations of presence and by the functions of writing and recording, it remains to be established what its particular purpose is. Through the transformations of presence, the mobile phone makes it possible, in the most varied situations, to perform *acts* that are essentially acts of speech and writing; these acts involve recording and therefore produce an *inscription*, which fixes the contingency of the act in the persistence of an object. This object, constituted as a *written act*, exists not only for the author of the act, but also for his current and potential interlocutors: in this sense it is a *social object* (see Ferraris 2005, p. 154). If I make a phone call to make an appointment, I will be obliged to respect it; if I send a text message to reserve a seat at the cinema, I will have the right to get it and the duty to pay for it. Social reality – with its "immense invisible ontology" (Searle 1995) made up of laws and banknotes, graduations and marriages, companies and nations – of course existed long before the invention of the mobile phone; however the mobile phone is a formidable constructor of social reality, because by extending the field of presence and writing, it gives us the possibility of producing recorded acts, and therefore social objects, everywhere and at any time. This tool, which we have characterized as a "Heideggerian machine" that transforms our mode of presence, and then as a "Derridean machine" that writes and records, finally reveals itself as a "Searlian machine" that offers us the possibility of synthesizing acts and inscriptions generating social objects, no matter where we are.

2. The ontology of film

"Ontology of film" is a discipline that seeks to answer three different questions: 1) What kind of object is the film? 2) What is the relationship between film and reality? 3) What mode of existence can be attributed to the fictional entities represented in the film? Theories of cinema have traditionally treated these issues jointly, answering question (1) through question (2) or through question (3). Realist theories have tried to answer the question about the specificity of the film by appealing to the privileged relationship between film and reality (Bazin, Kracauer, Cavell). Constructivist theories instead focus on the construction of a fictional dimension (Arnheim, Balázs). The semiotic variants of the latter theories have been summed up by Metz in the claim that cinema turns the world into discourse (1968). These theoretical options have been challenged by the advent of digital technologies, which on the one hand have raised the issue of the relationship between cinema and reality – which had been seemingly solved by the panlogism of semiotics – and on the other have showed the insufficiency of a "naive" realistic approach, focused exclusively on the material properties of the film.

Recently, we have witnessed the attempt to address the digital both in a realistic key (Rodowick *The Virtual Life of Film*) and in a constructivist key (Manovich's *The Language of New Media*); these proposals are however marked by the confusion between historiography and ontology, so that the descriptions of contingent singularities of the contemporary media scene are improperly promoted to the rank of essential properties of the film. For example, based on the developments of digital animation and video art, Manovich (2001, p. 308) draws the hyperbolic conclusion that "cinema becomes a particular branch of painting", whereas Rodowick (2008, p. 164) takes the photos of the Abu Ghraib prison to support the general thesis that digital images put us in contact with the reality of history.

Parallel to the advent of digital production, the theoretical debate was marked by the analytical philosophy of cinema: the writings of Noël Carroll and Gregory Currie constitute an unprecedented attack on the two great dogmas of traditional theories, the realist dogma of the photographic medium (for which cinema records the trace of reality on film), and the constructivist dogma of language or code (for which cinema transforms the world into discourse through a system of conventions). The arguments proposed by Currie (1993) and Carroll (1996, 2008) against the medium and the code made it difficult to answer the ontological question "what is the film?" in a realist way (the film is a reproduction of reality) or in a constructivist way (the film is a linguistic construction). The time had come to tackle the essential ontological question – what kind of object is the film? – directly, without detours or shortcuts. Starting from this awareness, Carroll identifies five conditions "individually necessary and jointly sufficient" (2008: 54) to define the film-object:

1) the "detached display", for which the space of the film is separate from the viewer's space;
2) the possibility of the impression of movement;
3) the fact that the performance-token (projections) of the work-type are generated by a template (the copy) which is in turn a token (a copy, that is, one of many occurrences);
4) the fact that the performance-token (projection) is not itself a work of art;
5) two-dimensionality.

The points (2) and (5) identify the main features of the film, which essentially consists of a series of two-dimensional images that give the viewer the impression of movement. The other three points have the function of neutralizing some insidious objections: point (1) serves to distinguish the film from the mirror, which also shows us two-dimensional images in motion, but in a space linked to our own space (the same goes for videogames, which show us a space conditioned by our own movement); the points (3) and (4) serve to distinguish the film from the theatre and above all from that singular "two-dimensional theatre" of shadow puppetry.

Technicalities aside, Carroll's answer to the ontological question "what is the film?" is basic and essential: a series of two-dimensional images that elicit the impression of movement. This definition may be – and has been –

criticized for its elementarity, which at first seems to fall into obviousness, truism. But precisely because of its simplicity, Carroll's definition provides an effective criterion to establish – without resorting to the cumbersome concepts of "remediation", "relocation", "multimedia convergence" – whether we are faced with a film object (e.g. video clips, TV series, mobile movies) or we are dealing with something else (e.g. videogames, interactive sites, slideshows). Historiographically, the mobile movie can be described as an evolution, a "remediation" or a "re-location" of the film, but ontologically it is *essentially a film*, with the same ontological dignity as Murnau's *Nosferatu* or Coppola's *Godfather*.

3. *The ontology of the mobile movie: transformations of presence*

Having clarified what we mean by film, we can now return to the ontology of the mobile phone, and reconsider its peculiar features (transformation of presence, writing, recording, construction of social reality) in order to identify the specifics of the mobile movie. First of all, as we mentioned, the ontology of the mobile phone is characterized by the transformations of presence induced by an object that is exclusively mine (*Jemeinigkeit*), that is always with me, ready at hand (*Zuhandenheit*), and that involves me emotionally (*Befindlichkeit*). Since this object is also a camera, it implies the possibility of filming personally (*Jemeinigkeit*), in any situation (*Zuhandenheit*), and with emotional involvement (*Befindlichkeit*). So if the mobile phone makes me *always available*, allowing me to always answer the ontological question "where are you?", the mobile movie goes a step further and makes me *always filming and filmable*, allowing me not only to say "where I am", but also to show it. This is an even more complete ubiquity, since even in those exceptional situations in which there is no reception, the phone still works as a video camera: the absence of reception prevents me from speaking but does not prevent me from filming. The exclusive, "always mine" nature of the mobile phone (*Jemeinigkeit*) allows me to show you exactly what I have seen; its being "at hand" (*Zuhandenheit*) allows me to show it to you in any situation; its being emotionally situated (*Befindlichkeit*) allows me to show it to you through my subjective participation. Thus defined, the mobile movie is not only close to science fiction devices of movies like *Death Watch*, *Brainstorm* and *Strange Days*, but also represents the extreme evolution of eight millimeter cameras and video cameras. Indeed, it turns any citizen into a potential Abraham Zapruder, the Dallas tailor who on the morning of 22nd

November 1963 took his camera to film the presidential parade, ending up immortalizing the assassination of John Kennedy. Any citizen indeed: it is no longer a matter of leaving home with the intention of filming something (albeit a parade rather than an assassination) and with an instrument that serves specifically to film; it is now a question of leaving home and having the possibility of filming, regardless of the specific will to do so. I bring a camera if I decide to make a movie, but the phone is always with me, regardless.

4. *The ontology of mobile movie: writing*

The mobile phone, as we have seen, serves to write in the literal sense that it has a keyboard with which you can produce texts. But with this keyboard you also decide when the movie you are shooting starts and when it ends, and you control its parameters (exposure, light, zoom). More generally, fitting perfectly in one hand and being under the full control of the hand (again, Heidegger's *Zuhandenheit*) the mobile phone can be plausibly compared to a pen transcribing the images of the things that surround us. The metaphor of the caméra-stylo, introduced in 1948 by Alexandre Astruc, has never been so pertinent. However, the point is no longer to claim the artistic nature of cinema and therefore its being "a language, that is, a form in which and through which an artist can express his own thought, however abstract, or translate his obsessions exactly as happens today in essays and novels" (Astruc 1992) – a language where writing would only be a subordinate component. Instead, it is a matter of regarding the camera, i.e. the mobile phone, essentially as a writing instrument, a pen, with which to take note, keep track, record, film and sign, well beyond the artistic intention of "expressing one's thought, however abstract, or translating one's obsessions exactly as happens today in essays and novels".

Still, this "stylo" has its own style, that is, a series of traits that characterize its mode of writing. The mobile movie is in this sense the most basic cinematic style, in which there is no screenplay, the set design is supplied by the environment and the acting depends on the potential human presence in that same environment, while cinematography typically is in low resolution and strongly determined by ambient light, the sound is exclusively recorded live, and editing is not required. Of the multiple components of the practice of filmmaking, the mobile movie retains only one, the most essential: framing. In its essentiality, the mobile movie is comparable to two other forms of "basic cinema": on the one hand the first films, in particular the vues Lumiére; on the other surveillance videos. But it is precisely thanks to this comparison that one can grasp the specificity of the mobile movie: the shots of the vues Lumiére screenings, like those produced by surveillance cameras, are characterized by fixity and objectivity, whereas the filming made with the mobile phone is characterised by subjectivity and by a mobile point of view.

The vues Lumiére and surveillance videos relate to a traditional framing concept such that the still shot is the basic option while movement is a further possibility specially designed by the technical device that supports it (camera dolly, steadicam, etc.). In the case of the mobile phone the situation is completely reversed: the basic option is the hand-held camera, while the still shot is given as an additional and exceptional possibility. The mobile phone is not meant to be still, it is meant to be hand-held; also because, unlike traditional cameras, it allows you to control the framing on the monitor, without having to look at the viewfinder: as happens with real writing, the eye merely controls the moving hand. These stylistic properties of the mobile movie bring us, once again, to the Heideggerian features of the mobile phone: it is ready at hand (*Zuhandenheit*), so that the framing is moving; it is always mine (*Jemeinigkeit*) and emotionally situated (*Befindlichkeit*), so that the framing – shaky like a signature – is essentially determined by the subject's point of view and emotional involvement.

5. Ontology of the mobile movie: recording

When we use the mobile phone for filming, what exactly are we doing? We are watching what we are filming, but we are also filming what we are watching. The mobile movie is based on the coordinated movement of eyes and hand, on the shifting gaze between the space you want to film and the display that depicts that space. What is produced in this act is essentially the recording of an experience: the trace of something I have experienced, seen and heard (namely the *Jemeinigkeit*, the exclusivity of experience), and at the same time the way in which I saw and heard it (namely the *Befindlichkeit*, the emotional situation). In the mobile movie, a perceptual flow is recorded and therefore delimited, isolated, outlined: it is subtracted from the irreversible flow of time and capitalized into a segment of ideally infinite iterability. In this sense, the recording that constitutes a mobile movie is to the immediacy of perception what writing proper is to the immediacy of the spoken words: the mobile movie and writing are both

Derridean traces that betray the authenticity and fullness of presence, but they also guarantee its persistence and reveal its differential structure.

Thus defined, the mobile movie can be understood as a transcription of a "tranche de vie": a film composed of a single long shot, of reduced duration, which warrants the rendering and preservation of an experience. We obviously do not mean to argue that recording a "tranche de vie" is all that can be achieved with a mobile phone: nothing prevents a ruthless filmmaker from using a mobile phone to shoot a film with a screenplay, set design and actors (as for example Jean-Charles Fitoussi's *Nocturnes pour le roi de Rome*). At the same time, nothing prevents the film made with a mobile phone from being uploaded into a post-production software system for manipulation, editing and mixing; indeed, even sticking to the technology of the mobile phone it is possible to make a rudimentary editing, for example by using the pause button to temporarily stop the shot, or alternating the point of view of the "internal camera" (the front-facing one) and the point of view of the "external camera". Yet all these possibilities go beyond the domain of the mobile movie: they are attempts to adapt its specific form, determined by the ontology of the mobile phone, to the practice of traditional cinematography. This "forced use" of the mobile phone can be justified with the intention of producing a cinematic work using the most basic and popular tool, available both to a director and to the most ordinary spectator, just like a pen or a word processor are used by novelists and readers alike; in this sense, think of mobile movies such as *SMS Sugar Man* by Aryan Kaganof or *La paura* by Pippo Delbono (cf. the essays by Amaducci and Buquicchio in Ambrosini-Maina-Marcheschi 2009).

However, the main characteristic of the mobile movie remains the material trace of a tranche de vie: a block of space-time taken away from time, a perceptual experience deposited in an audiovisual segment. This is shown precisely in those narrative films that resort to fictional mobile movies to intensify the reality effect: think of the videos shot by soldiers in Paul Haggis's *In the Valley of Elah*, or the images of a man committing suicide in M. Night Shyamalan's *The Happening*. A film shot with a mobile phone testifies to something that happened, and even when what is filmed does not correspond exactly to what you see (for example when you point the phone towards yourself, or when you use it as a periscope raising your arm in the middle of crowd, see Ferraris 2005, p. 99), the mobile movie still represents what you listen to: it captures an atmosphere and transcribes a presence, returning the trace of a lived experience.

6. *Ontology of the mobile movie: social reality*

We have seen that the mobile movie surrogates a perceptive experience just as writing proper surrogates a thought content. In carrying out this vicarious function, the mobile movie shares two essential traits with writing: exteriority and persistence. Filming with a mobile phone is therefore an act that produces an inscription, which can be considered a social object to the extent that it concerns not only the one who produced it by recording what one saw and heard, but also those who will see it and hear it. Filming with a mobile phone means recording one's own experience and offering it to the perception of others: I record what I see and what I feel for others to see and hear. In this sense, the mobile movie transforms an individual and private experience into a social object. It is also true that there are films shot with the mobile phone for the use and consumption of the author himself, but even in this case the recorded experience is potentially accessible to a number of other viewers (from nosy people to detectives), though against the will of the author.

A more ordinary use, on the other hand, contemplates a range of options that allow the author to intentionally publish the recording of his experience by uploading it to the web, to the social networks. What changes, depending on the circumstances, it is only the number of real and potential interlocutors to whom the written act is addressed, but the constitutive purpose of the mobile movie is the same: the socialization of an experience.

7. *Conclusion*

The analytical ontology of cinema borrowed from Noël Carroll allowed us to break free from the dogmas of language and medium, and from the consequent quarrel between realists and constructivists. This has made it possible to address the mobile movie starting from a definition of film that is as neutral and hospitable as possible: a series of two-dimensional images that give the viewer the impression of movement. But now that we have identified the specifics of the mobile movie, we find ourselves faced with a somewhat paradoxical conclusion: the recovery of the realist option, which seemed definitively overcome by the advent of the digital and theoretically refuted by the analytical argument. In the age of digital dematerialization, the mobile movie re-proposes the most traditional of cinema ontologies, that is, the idea that the act of filming essentially consists in recording an event: in its mummification (Bazin), in its redemption (Kracauer), or even in an authentic view of this same event, a perspective directed from the present to the past, comparable to the posthumous images of the stars in the sky (Cavell). This apparent contradiction, however, is resolved considering that the ontology of the mobile movie circumscribes this realistic option: first of all it does not extend it to the totality of cinema, avoiding a number of objections (what about editing? and soundtrack? and special effects? and animation movies? and computer graphics?). Moreover, the image of reality offered by the mobile phone does not consist in an objective and univocal reproduction, but rather in rendering an experience that is indelibly marked by a subjective point of view. The mobile movie thus identifies a peculiar mode of ontological realism, which in turn reveals a peculiar modality of a wider and more comprehensive ontology of the film.

To grasp the specific realism of the mobile movie in its fullness, let's try to conceive a simple thought experiment. Imagine a hypothetical mobile phone that can only be used by its owner and that encodes videos in a "proprietary format" that only allows for their reproduction, but not their modification. We would have a perfect eyewitness: an instrument that guarantees the veracity of what it says ("on that date, at that time, the person recorded that situation"). The only possible counterfeiting would be to manipulate the filmed scene, for example by staging a false aggression. However, even in this case our ideal mobile phone would not lie: it would be misleading, but in good faith, and could not be accused of false testimony. The sincerity of its account is rooted in its idiomaticity, that is, in the causal link that connects a text to its genesis. Precisely because of this gift of idiomaticity, writing – under certain circumstances – is valid as an ontological proof: as a signature, as an autograph, as a guarantee of continuity with its origin (see Ferraris 2005, p. 267). In the case of the mobile movie, we are dealing with a double origin: the event filmed and the presence of the person who filmed it. The world and the hand write together the text of the film. Filming with a mobile phone involves a double signature.

Bibliographical references

Ambrosini, M., Maina, G., Marcheschi, E., ed by, *I film in tasca. Videofonino, cinema e televisione*, Ghezzano (Pi), Felici, 2009
Astruc, A., *Du stylo à la caméra... et de la caméra au stylo: écrits (1942-1948)*, Paris, L'Archipel, 1992
Carroll, N. and Choi, J., ed. by, *Philosophy of Film and Motion Pictures: An Anthology*, Oxford, Blackwell, 2006

Carroll, N., *Defining the Movie Image* (1996), in Carroll and Choi 2006

Carroll, N., *The Philosophy of Motion Pictures*, Oxford, Blackwell, 2008

Currie, G., *The Long Goodbye: The Imaginary Language of Film* (1993), in Carroll and Choi 2006

Ferraris, M., *Dove sei? Ontologia del telefonino*, Milano, Bompiani, 2005

Ferraris, M., *Documentalità. Perché è necessario lasciar tracce*, Bari, Laterza, 2009

Manovich, L., *The language of new media*, Cambridge Mass./London, The MIT Press, 2001

Menicocci, G., *Cinefonino. Le immagini al telefono si muovono on line*, "close up", n° 22, 2007

Metz, C. *Essais sur la signification au cinéma*, Paris, Editions Klincksieck, 1968

Rodowick, D. N., *The Virtual Life of Film*, Boston, Harvard University Press, 2007

Searle, J. R., *The Construction of Social Reality*, New York, Free Press, 1995

2.
FILM ME, STUPID
Notes on a Logocentric "Bustina"

Umberto Eco's "Bustina di minerva" published on 10 July 2012 (http://espresso.repubblica.it/dettaglio/stupido-metti-via-quel-telefonino/2185815/18) has a vehement title, "Stupid, put that mobile phone away", and a summary that adequately clarifies its meaning: "We film or photograph, and then maybe upload everything on the Internet. Nowadays many people do not think of anything else when attending an event. And so they forget what is really happening right there and then". In the article, Umberto Eco supports his criticism with four paradigmatic cases, derived from personal experience.

The first two examples are ones in which Eco is the victim of reproduction devices: "I was trying to talk at the Spanish Academy in Rome, but I was blinded by the flash of a lady's phone"; "in San Leo, during a wonderful public initiative ro rediscover the landscapes that appear in Piero della Francesca's paintings, three people were busy photographing me instead." What Eco is struck by, in addition to the flash, is that "in both cases the people were not a trash TV kind of crowd, but presumably educated people who had come to attend a cultural event." And yet these "presumably educated" individuals had regressed to the level of a "trash TV kind of crowd" because they had "chosen not to *understand* what was being said in order to *memorize* with their phone something that they could have *seen* with their own eyes" (italics added).

Eco's explanation for this anthropological devolution is based on two implicit assumptions. The first is that participation in cultural events is symptomatic of an evolutionary level that is markedly higher than that of television viewers. This statement is already questionable, but let's accept this point for now, so as to focus on his second assumption: the idea that understanding is the primal human activity, while memorization is something stupidly mechanical, which brings one to the level of a machine (through which one performs the stupid operation of memorization) or an animal (to whose cognitively poor condition, devoid of understanding, one thus regresses).

By clearly distinguishing between understanding and memorization, Eco excludes that memorization may somehow constitute the condition of understanding, whose genuine antecedent is instead identified in the act of "seeing with one's own eyes". Eco's axiology, which explicitly opposes (good) communication and (bad) recording, is therefore based on an implicit epistemology that directly connects perception and understanding, and conceives memorization as purely accessory (or even harmful when, as happens in the case of mobile phones, it overtakes the higher functions of perceiving and understanding).

This epistemology, however, does not account for the fact – repeatedly highlighted in the history of philosophy, from Aristotle to Derrida – that "perceptions and thoughts present themselves as inscriptions in our mind" (Ferraris, *Documentalità*, 2009, p. 361). That is to say that our mind, in exercising the functions of perceiving and understanding, behaves just like a tabula, a tablet (cf. Ferraris, *Anima e I-Pad*, 2011), or a mobile phone (cf. Ferraris, *Ontologia del telefonino*, 2005), that is, as a memory device. So, in severely reprimanding the people filming with the mobile phone and inviting them to turn it off in order to see for themselves, Eco is simply advising them to use *another mobile phone*, the one inside their head. It may well be that this "built-in phone" works better than other models – indeed, in many ways, it seems that for now it is the case – but anyhow the controversy loses its philosophical connotation, moving on a level parallel to the economic-technological competition between telephone companies or hardware producers.

This unforeseen outcome sheds new light on the two final examples of the "Bustina", in which Eco is no longer the passive victim of "telephone harassment" but is the active subject of the experience. The first example concerns a trip to the French cathedrals, in 1960, during which a 28-year-old Eco took photos "like a madman" and then realized that he had not actually seen anything. Here the author is being self-critical, equating his young self to today's mobile phone brutes, but also indicates the path of repentance: "I threw away the camera and in my subsequent trips I *recorded* what I saw only *mentally*" (italics added). Once again, axiology is based on epistemology, but as we have already noted, "recording only mentally" is anything but innocent, both because it is constitutive of perceiving as well as of understanding, and because its iterative structure is the same as that of recording devices. Throwing away the camera to record only mentally, in short, does not mean being more human or more intelligent: it only means throwing away an "external" camera and replacing it with another that is inside our head.

The final example goes further back in time. Now it's 1943 and we meet an 11-year-old Eco, displaced after the bombings. The scene he witnesses is even more excruciating than the atrocities of the ongoing war: "a truck had hit a cart driven by a farmer with his wife, the woman had been thrown to the ground, her head had split and she lay in a puddle of blood and brain substance (in my memory, still horrified, it was as if they had squashed a cream and strawberry cake) while her husband held her tightly, howling with despair." This time, however, young Eco's behaviour is impeccable and exemplary: no photos, no cameras, no mobile phones, only gaze and thought, and then, later, memory and words. While admitting that the technological backwardness of the time also helped, Eco declares to be proud of his conduct: "What would have happened if I had, as happens today to every kid, a phone with a built-in camera? Maybe I would have recorded it, to show friends that I was there, and then I would have uploaded my visual capital on YouTube [...] Instead I kept everything in my memory, and that image, seventy years later, continues to obsess me and to educate me – to make me a non-indifferent participant in the pain of others".

Here Eco does not merely reaffirm the initial thesis that on the one hand there are bad representations (the "visual capital") recorded by technological devices, and on the other there are good representations preserved in one's inner self. In addition, Eco suggests that there can be a good representation also in the external world, outside the intimacy of the mind. This "good representation" is linguistic. In fact, unlike the image, language does not replace thought but expresses it. In short, this is not a thesis of radical non-representability, like that of Adorno, for whom "To write poetry after Auschwitz is barbaric", or like that of the early Wittgenstein, for whom "Whereof one cannot speak, thereof one must be silent". For Eco the act of barbarism cannot be the representation as such, because a tragic event can be represented adequately in terms of a linguistic description ("a truck had hit a cart driven by a farmer with his wife...") which, moreover, does not disdain rhetorical figures ("it was as if they had squashed a cream and strawberry cake"). The act of barbarism is only given if this representation takes place outside language, in the domain of cameras, video cameras and mobile phones.

In this way, Wittgenstein's logoclastic saying "Whereof one cannot speak, thereof one must be silent" is reversed in its logocentric opposite: "Whereof one should not photograph and film, thereof one must speak". But then the controversy against filming mobile phones presupposes not only a questionable theory of the mind, by which understanding takes priority over memorization, but also a very dubious theory of representation, for which language overtakes the technically reproduced image, as if language were not itself a technique – as if language were instead an emanation of the spirit.

To raise the stakes a little, one could hypothesize that, faced with the now evident failure of the great semiological project to reduce every form of representation to the paradigm of the linguistic sign, its proponents are left with the desperate move of labelling as stupid and immoral the forms of representation that cannot be attributed to this paradigm. A technically reproduced image is stupid as such, while language is intelligent as such: this seems to be the final claim of semiotics, which reveals that it never really cut the cord that binds it to idealism and the philosophy of spirit, as Derrida points out in "The Pit and the Pyramid: Introduction to Hegel's Semiology" (in *Margins of Philosophy*, 1972). Going back even further in the history of philosophy, one realizes that Eco here regards mobile phones, photography and cinema as Plato regarded writing in *Phaedrus*: as an impure surrogate of thought, which risks compromising the purity of thought itself, as Derrida points out in "Plato's Pharmacy" (in *Dissemination*, 1972). This condemnation of the images "written" by the mobile phone, the photo camera or the video camera, however, is a semi-ironic and almost paradoxical move for semiotics, if we consider that the programmatic intent of this field of study consisted precisely in dealing with human culture and every aspect of it, without idealistic prejudices, regardless of canons and hierarchies.

Language is intelligent, pictures are stupid. Yet you can easily find a number of clever uses of depiction (think of Capa, Cartier-Bresson, Rossellini, Godard), and even more easily a lot of stupid or infamous uses of language (no need to make examples). Why, then, should we let our value judgments be determined by an axiology of forms of representation – intelligent language, stupid pictures – rather than evaluating single representative acts? Why could there not be pictures, even made with the mobile phone, and even uploaded on Youtube, which "make us non-indifferent participants in the pain of others"? And why, symmetrically, could there not be linguistic descriptions that remain indifferent to the tragedy of the events described, preferring to indulge in some stupid rhetorical gimmicks? The image can be intelligent, and language can be stupid. There seems to be no decisive reason to deny these possibilities, outside the idealistic prejudices of our cultural tradition. In this sense, the best answer to Eco's logocentric imperative – "stupid, put that mobile phone away" – comes from a movie hero, the *idiot savant* Forrest Gump, with his crypto-behaviorist motto that could have come out of the later Wittgenstein: "stupid is as stupid does".

ANIMALS

1.
HUMAN, ANIMAL, MACHINE
Anthropocentrism and Science Fiction Cinema

First, we will show how the reduction (or removal) of animality in the anthropocentric discourse often goes hand in hand with that of machinality. Then, we will consider science fiction as a cinematic space in which anthropocentrism is questioned by re-evaluating these dimensions that are normally reduced (or removed). Finally, we will discuss the possibility of drawing a new, more generous anthropological perspective on the animal and the machine from science fiction cinema.

1. *Machines*

In an influential text[1], Richard Rorty splits up Western philosophical doctrines into *a Kantian line* that searches for the universal structures of thought, and a *Hegelian line* that instead conceives of thought as essentially determined by history. In dealing with animality and machinenality, we can outline an alternative distinction: on the one hand *a Cartesian line* that relates thought to the radical diversity of man from the animal and the machine (assimilated under the category of soulless mechanicism); on the other hand, *a Leibnizian line* which tries to understand thought precisely starting from man's bond with the non-human. This distinction changes the situation depicted by Rorty: the heirs of Descartes, in fact, include not only "Kantian" philosophers such as Husserl and Searle, who reformulate the cogito in terms of consciousness and intentionality; but also "Hegelian" philosophers such as Heidegger and Gadamer, who tend to identify thought with the language of the spirit, thus denying both the animal and the machine the possibility of authentic thought.

---

1   R. Rorty, *Contingency, Irony, and Solidarity*, Cambridge University Press, New York, 1989.

Who are Leibniz's heirs? First of all, the most radical Enlightenment philosophers such as La Mettrie, who in the *Man A Machine* reaffirms, and at the same time overturns, the Cartesian position: the animal is indeed a machine, but man is in turn essentially an animal and therefore a machine; the differences are only quantitative, the ontological substance is the same. The contiguity between man and animal was strongly reaffirmed also by Darwinian evolutionism, while on the side of machines Turing's research made plausible the idea that a machine can somehow think, and therefore pass a test that would make it indistinguishable from a human being. In the contemporary debate, we find the "Leibnizian" approach both in neuroscience, which is trying to localize the thought processes in the brain[2], and on the side of the so-called strong artificial intelligence theorists, for whom thought processes could be performed by computer programs. These are logical-scientific positions that Rorty would call "Kantian", but the issue of the animal and the machine produces philosophical results of great importance also on the side of the "Hegelians". In particular in the writings of Derrida, the criticism of logocentrism is given in terms of a downsizing of language, consciousness and intentionality (i.e. the specificity of human thought), and symmetrically of a re-evaluation of writing, and more generally of memory and the trace (that is, the dimensions that human thought has in common with the "thought" of animals and machines)[3].

Derrida's reflections on animality and machinality find significant correspondences in the analyzes that the artificial intelligence theorist Douglas Hofstadter devotes to two famous mental experiments that are also, in their own way, science-fiction tales: Searle's Chinese room and Nagel's bat[4]. Let's start with the first one. To prove that a machine cannot think, Searle imagines a room in which there is a man who speaks only

---

2   The title of Antonio Damasio's book is emblematic: *Descartes' Error: Emotion, Reason, and the Human Brain*, Quill, New York, 1994

3   While the Derridean apology of animality is famous and often cited (see *The animal that therefore I am*, 1997), the reflection on machineness is less known, despite being full of ideas. Consider, for example, this quote which comes in handy to complete a deconstruction of Hegel's critique of Leibniz:"What Hegel, the relevant interpreter of the whole history of philosophy, *could never think* is a machine that would work. That would work without, to this extent, being governed by an order of reappropriation."(from *Margins of Philosophy*, University of Chicago Press, 1982, p.107).

4   J. Searle, *Minds, Brains and Programs* (1980); T. Nagel, *What Is it Like to Be a Bat?* (1974). Both essays are quoted and discussed in Douglas Hofstadter in *The Mind's I: Fantasies and reflections on self and soul* edited by D. Hofstadter, D. Dennett, Bantam Books, New York, 1981.

English and not Chinese, but is able to manipulate Chinese symbols based on rules written in English on some sheets of paper. This man receives from the outside, from people who speak Chinese, a series of sheets containing questions written in Chinese, to which he answers with new sheets written in Chinese but obtained by manipulating Chinese symbols according to the rules written in English. Although the answers that the man in the room gives to the outside appear sensible to those who receive them, he does not really understand their meaning: he has only suitably combined symbols according to the rules.

For Searle, this is precisely the situation of Turing's intelligent computer, which does not really understand human language even though it uses it impeccably; the machine lacks intentionality, which is a specific property of the brain, a "demon" that only the brain is able to generate. Criticizing Searle's mental experiment, Hofstadter argues instead that "nearly all of the understanding must lie in the billions of symbols on paper, and practically none of it in the demon"[5], and that therefore intentionality and conscience are not faculties that are added to the manipulation of symbols (i.e. inscriptions) on the basis of rules (that is, other inscriptions): intentionality and conscience are the mode of manipulation of inscriptions when it reaches levels of high complexity.

This apology of machinality is linked to the question of animality, as shown by Hofstadter's discussion of the essay *What Is it Like to Be a Bat?*, in which Nagel investigates the possible subjective experience the animal may have and concludes that it is inaccessible to us: "in contemplating the bats we are in much the same position that intelligent bats or Martians would occupy if they tried to form a conception of what it was like to be us"[6]. Critically analyzing Nagel's mental experiment, Hofstadter shows that it implies not only the possibility that animals think, but also that machines do: subjectivity is essentially linked to the ownership of a "point of view", and the link that exists between "having a point of view" and "being a

---

5   *Ibid*, p. 375. Ferraris's criticism of Searle follows the same line, albeit from an explicitly Derridean perspective: "On closer inspection, the thought Searle refers to is nothing more than the dream of a living spirit – as the theoreticians of the nineteenth-century science of the spirit would have put it – that dwells in man's head unlike what happens in computers. Now, we can certainly say that we seem to think, whereas we do not know if computers or animals think, but it is a fact that we represent our mind (and not just computers) as a writing surface, like a tabula" (M. Ferraris, *Ricostruire la decostruzione. Cinque saggi a partire da Derrida*, Bompiani, Milano, 2010, pp. 95-96).

6   In *The Mind's I*, edited by D. Hofstadter, D. Dennett, cit., p.395.

representational system" allows one to identify sentient and thinking beings "with physical representational systems with sufficient richness in their repertoire of categories and sufficiently well-indexed memories of their world-lines"[7]. But these "physical representational systems" able to realize a "point of view" can be human beings, animals and machines, without any ontological priority being granted to the first.

2. Science fiction: the beginning

What is it like to be an animal? What does it mean to be a machine? What distinguishes human beings from non-human animals and machines? These questions, which are the core of both Derrida's reflections and Searle's and Nagel's mental experiments discussed by Hofstadter, run through the history of science fiction cinema. Unlike what happens in literary science fiction, which mostly tends to build sophisticated narrative mechanisms and refined metaphysical conjectures, science fiction cinema has always distinguished itself for a certain degree of brutality. In this sense, one can understand its proximity to the horror genre. While literary science fiction was launching into fascinating speculations on remote galaxies and future civilizations, science fiction cinema was consumed in its obsession with animality and machinality, taking as its main – not to say only – theme the possibility that the animal and the machine are right at the edges of humanity, infiltrating it, turning out to be an essential part of the human being.

In the prehistory of the genre, from silent cinema to early sound movies, animality and machineness already dominated the scene: on the one hand *Metropolis* (F. Lang, 1927) represents the automaton as a disturbing double of the human, on the other *King Kong* (E. Schoedsack and M. Cooper, 1933) unleashes the devastating power of the beast. With these two masterpieces, machinality and animality imposed themselves as essential coordinates of science-fiction cinema, which would obsessively continue to stage variations on the theme of the anthropomorphic automaton and the great ape. At the heart of the most evolved human civilization (*King Kong*'s New York and the imaginary city of *Metropolis*) there is still something uncivilized and non-human: a form of life that not only is opposed to the human, but somehow shares its deepest essence.

---

7   *Ibid*, p. 411.

In *King Kong*, the ape climbing on skyscrapers is not only the *object* of people's panic as well as of airplane attacks, but also the *subject* of both its own gaze (which the film highlights with a series of subjective shots) and feelings (addressed to the female character). Similarly, *Metropolis* represents the automaton as a double negative of the heroine Maria and more generally as an antagonist of human civilization, but at the same time gives it an erotic element (see the scene in the nightclub) and a political determination (see the speech to the workers) that make it paradoxically more human than its human counterpart, as demonstrated by the fact that the performance of the actress Brigitte Helm is much more vivid and convincing in the role of the machine than in the mannered and artificial interpretation of the girl.

Science fiction cinema thus has always had a fundamental duality, ever since its earliest days: on the one hand, on the surface, the science fiction narrative is about how the human resists, almost always victoriously, to the threats coming from animality and machinality; on the other hand, on a deeper level, man, animal and machine find themselves sharing something more essential than their differences and conflicts. Recalling the distinctions introduced above, we can thus say that science fiction tells "Cartesian" stories (how man defeats the animal and the machine) but they often reveal a "Leibnizian" implication (how man is structurally akin to the animal and the machine that apparently oppose him). One of the key figures in this sense is mutation, which dominates the horror science fiction scene of the 1930s. Films such as *Dr. Jekyll and Mr. Hyde* (R. Mamoulian, 1931) and *Doctor X* (M. Curtiz, 1932) represent technological manipulations that bring out the animal roots of man, while *Frankenstein* (J. Whale, 1931) and *Island of Lost Souls* (E. Kenton, 1933) portray sorts of human beings who are created as artifacts by manipulating corpses and animals through technical procedures. At the center of these films, there is a mutating humanity that owes its being to machinality and finds its destiny in animality.

3. *Science fiction: the middle*

With the great sci-fi boom of the 1950s, the figures of the animal and the machine were projected onto the figures of the alien and the spaceship. The extraterrestrial creature was typically represented with two essential traits: technological rationality (which allowed it to construct sophisticated spaceships with which it reached our planet) and animal brutality (which prevents it from any dialogic and collaborative relationship with human civilization). Emblematic titles in this sense include *The Thing from Another World* (C. Nyby, 1951), in which the alien is presented as a sort of hominid carried around by a flying saucer, and above all *The War of the Worlds* (B. Haskin, 1953), which represents aliens by insisting on their animality and machinality: they have a visual system "like a television camera" (consisting of three viewers: one red, one green and one blue) installed on a reptile body, and they move inside hyper-technological spacecraft with the animal features of a manta ray.

Projected on the figure of the alien (which etymologically means other than human) animality and machineness seem to position themselves at a "Cartesian" distance that is all in all reassuring: even if the aliens are hostile and destructive, they represent an entirely external threat that threatens the contingent existence of humanity but not its metaphysical essence. The alien is the Other identified by animality and machinality, the Other that humanity is called to defeat in order to reaffirm its essence. However, even science fiction based on extraterrestrial invaders often offers a second level of reading, so that the radical otherness of the alien-animal-machine turns out to be much closer to the human essence than one might think.

This idea is particularly explicit in films that insist on the theme of the body snatcher, that is, the human infiltrated by the alien and mutated into a kind of automaton: for example, *It Came from Outer Space* (J. Arnold 1953), *Invaders from Mars* (W. Menzies, 1953), *Invasion of the Body Snatchers* (D. Siegel, 1956). A similar situation, of apparent opposition but underlying correlation between man, animal and machine, is found in films that represent the combination of technology and animality as the origin of monstrous creatures: the giant ants of *Them!* (G. Douglas, 1954), the hypertrophic spiders of *Tarantula* (J. Arnold, 1955), or the telepathic crabs of *Attack of the Crab Monsters* (R. Corman, 1957).

The most emblematic title from this perspective is undoubtedly *The Fly* (K. Neumann, 1958), in which the mutations of animals (a cat, a hamster) caused by technology are followed by the much more shocking mutation of man into a fly (and, in parallel, of a fly into a man) by means of a machine. But what does it mean to be a man-fly? One can attempt to answer by analyzing the scene in which the scientist's wife discovers the mutation of her husband: a first shot/countershot contrasting the woman's terrified reaction and the man-fly's monstrous face, followed by a second shot/countershot in which the camera first focuses on the monster's eye and then reveals the face of his screaming wife, multiplied and faceted by a vision system that is no longer human. The first shot/countershot merely presents the mutation as something monstrous, but the second one gives us the mutant's point of view, making us share his animality.

4. *Science fiction: the end*

In the 1960s the science fiction imaginary was taken over by the intellectualism of auteur cinema, but the themes of animality and machinality remained central, finding an emblematic representation in the cut with which *2001: A Space Odyssey* (S. Kubrick, 1968) connects the bone thrown by the ape with the spaceship dancing in the cosmos. In Kubrick's vision, human civilization is nothing but the link between the animal and the machine, and this essential correlation is resolved in a circular and nihilistic narration: the history of technology inaugurated by the ape ends with the madness of the computer that regresses to animal instincts, proving that the common foundation of humanity, animality and machineness consists in a blind and fierce will to power.

It is customary to say, with good reason, that after *2001: A Space Odyssey* science fiction cinema became "adult", so in the following decades the threats that animality and machineness bring to human existence took on ever more disturbing and insidious forms. Humankind often seems about to succumb to animals (*Phase IV*, S. Bass, 1974) or machines (the robots of *Westworld*, M. Crichton, 1973). In Steven Spielberg's early films, this threat of annihilation of humanity is represented in outstanding essentiality by the killing machine of *Duel* (1971) and the killer animal of *Jaws* (1975), then finding more specifically genre-related declinations with the dinosaurs of *Jurassic Park* (1993) and with the aliens of *The War of The Worlds* (2005). The threat of the animal and the machine is equally at work in *Alien* (R. Scott, 1979), where humans are besieged by an alien monster that combines the most terrifying traits of both animality and machinality, while being submitted to the implacable logic of the computer Mother and the android Ash. Similarly, in *Predator* (J. McTiernan, 1987), humanity is prey to an alien hunter that combines an ape-like appearance with an impressive technological endowment (starting from the infrared viewer through which, once again, the human viewer is given the point of view of the alien-animal-machine).

But what is more important to note, for the purposes of the present argument, is that even in contemporary science fiction there is the double level of reading that we identified as the essential trait of both the "prehistoric" and "classical" phases of the genre. That is to say that there is not only a narrative surface level, which represents the "Cartesian" conflict between man and the powers of animality and machinality, but also a further level in which man, animal and machine are revealed to be correlated, in a "Leibnizian" way, by an essential link, deeper than their conflicts and differences.

This inextricable link between humanity, animality and machinality finds emblematic examples in some key works of the new science fiction: from *The Thing* (J. Carpenter, 1982), which combines the plot of *The Thing from Another World* with the theme of body-snatchers, so that the alien-animal-machine is indiscernible from the human; to *Avatar* (J. Cameron, 2009), which tells the new alliance between an automaton that makes up for the absence of man and an alien population with feline features: here the new stage of human evolution goes through the coupling of animality and machinality. The most original formulations of the link between animal and machine in contemporary cinema are found in David Cronenberg's films, a filmmaker accustomed to representing the human body as an entity essentially exposed to the intrusion of animals (*Shivers*, 1975, and *Rabid*, 1977) and machines (*Videodrome*, 1983 and *Crash*, 1996).

A paradigmatic film in this regard is *The Fly* (1986), a remake of the 1958 film that depicts the fusion not only of man and animal, but also of the machine. From this perspective, another crucial Cronenberg's work is *eXistenZ* (1999), which in contrast to the abstract and aseptic simulations of *Matrix* (A. and L. Wachowski, 1999) represents a virtual reality created by special bio-technological devices, the game pods; as one progresses in the game, game pods take on ever more animalistic features, and through them animality penetrates into the human body just as, through the ludic simulation, the machine penetrates the mind: once again the narration culminates in the genesis of a new creature that is no longer human or animal or machine, but man-animal-machine, inextricably joined.

5. *The virtuous brute*

The metaphysical hierarchy that prioritizes the "Cartesian" to the "Leibinizian" view (i.e. intentionality over automatism[8], consciousness

---

8   The distinction between intentionality and automatism has recently found an original reformulation, which highlights the affinities between man and animal, in the distinction between belief and alief proposed by the American philosopher Tamar Szabó Gendler in *Alief and Belief*, in "Journal of Philosophy" vol. 105 n. 10-2008, pp. 634-663

over intuition[9], language over inscription) often translates into an aesthetic and cultural hierarchy whereby true art and true culture are those that capture the essence of the human (that is, language, consciousness, intentionality) while the forms of representation that refer to man in his essential bonds with animality and machinality are – more or less explicitly – discredited. In this sense, the aesthetic prejudice that denies artistic legitimacy to films because of the mechanical component of the cinematic device[10] is similar to the critical prejudice that denies cultural legitimacy to science fiction narratives because they are based on "missiles and monsters" (that is, on machines and animals[11]).

On the contrary, the appreciation of cinema as an "artistic machine" and of science-fiction as an opening to the dimensions of animality and machinality, leads us to criticize the "Cartesian" premises of our culture in view of a more "Leibnizian" conception of our being. This conception that cultivates humanism while taking into account an irreducible basic brutality, which derives from man's essential connection with the "brute instinct" that philosophers attribute to animals and with the "brute calculation" that engineers attribute to machines. To put it with a Dantean-Leibnizian Ulysses of cinema and science fiction, we were indeed "form'd to live the life of brutes, *and* virtue to pursue and knowledge high".

9   "This 'basic intuition' is rooted in the senses (even though it overrides them) – and as such it has nothing to do with the supersensible intuition of the various eight- and nineteenth-century irrationalisms. It is widespread throughout the world, without geographical, historical, ethnic, sexual or class limits – and therefore it is far from any form of superior knowledge, the privilege of a chosen few. It is the heritage of the Bengalis deprived of their knowledge by Sir William Herschel; of hunters; of sailors; of women. It ties the human animal closely to other animal species", Carlo Ginzburg, *Spie. Radici di un paradigma indiziario* in *Miti emblemi spie. Morfologia e storia*, Einaudi, Torino, 1986, p. 193
10   A contemporary version of this argument is found in the writings of the philosopher Roger Scruton; see in particular *Photography and Representation* (1983) in *Philosophy of Film and Motion Pictures: An Anthology* ed. by N.Carroll, J. Choi, Blackwell, Oxford, 2006.
11   For a critical discussion of this prejudice, cf. L. Bandirali, E. Terrone, *Nell'occhio, nel cielo. Teoria e storia del cinema di fantascienza*, Lindau, Torino, 2008, pp. 99-100.

2.
CINEMA FOR CHILDREN AND ANIMALS

A very cultivated friend of mine once sent me an email in the middle of the night, advising me to go see *Inside Out* with my nine-year-old daughter. Too late: my daughter had already seen it with her mother, who is also a philosopher familiar with the role of emotions in reasoning and in practical decisions, and therefore had, so to speak, a professional interest in the matter. Gone is the time when parents would surprise you reading comics, hiding a report card.

What has happened, other than a generic "modern" becoming? On the one hand, now there are many generations that grew up with comics and cartoons (*The Yellow Kid*, the prototypical comic strip, dates back to 1894-95, the time of Nietzsche and Mahler), and therefore are able to recognize their merits (my first contact with the Divine Comedy was the comic version with Donald Duck as Dante and I do not remember what other duck as Virgil).

On the other hand, and above all, the market has recognized the enormous cognitive potentialities of a medium (drawing, whether fixed or moving) and of an audience: children. The two things do not necessarily go together, but when this happens there is an expressive miracle that could hardly be achieved in other areas. But the fundamental point, in my opinion, lies not simply in the medium, but in the recipients: the children.

Children are spontaneous metaphysicians. While adults generally focus on contingent and practical matters (even those rare adults who engage in metaphysics), children are open to truly radical questions: for example, if God is infinite, how can there be room for everything else? (a question that Saul Kripke, the greatest logician and ontologist of the past century, asked his mother when he was four years old).

Although the opposite is usually maintained, adults can be and are often lied to – children cannot. The subtle allusion in *Madame Bovary* ("she abandoned herself") becomes a concrete story of rape in *Little Red Riding Hood*. The smooth descriptions of the relations between servants and masters in the *Recherche* or the *Buddenbrooks* are replaced by the ruthless description of power relations in *Kung Fu Panda*. Children do not admit cultural excuses. A child will never be persuaded to watch Antonioni's *Red Desert* with the argument that it is a culturally relevant work. The reasons for seeing a film must lie in the film itself and not in the halo of cultural respectability that it may possibly evoke.

Children, above all, are relatively little interested in the *refugium peccatorum* that we call sex. A struggling screenwriter can always get by narrating another fifty shades of gray or some other colour. But it is easy to imagine the tears and great boredom that such a work would arouse in a movie theatre full of children and popcorn. Paradoxically, the only way to make *Fifty shades of gray* palatable to a child audience, and perhaps even to an adult audience (which is wider than you think), would be to make explicit the fable structure underlying it (*Cinderella*, in this case), and above all to make an animation movie of it.

In fact, animation movies do not merely offer caricatures of the human race. They do a lot more. They have narrative possibilities unthinkable for traditional cinema (what stuntman would accept to be chased by Wile E. Coyote?). Above all, they put the non-human animal, this great repressed of traditional fiction, in the foreground. Lions, gazelles, elephants, pandas, cats and mice are the true heroes of cartoons, while at most they are the background of cinema and of "realistic" storytelling.

So what is special about the animal, this being that feels closer to us in childhood than it does in adulthood? First of all, expressiveness. The human being can be anything, but the animal is something *par excellence*: strength or cunning, humility, shyness, sovereignty. Animals embody powers, more than characters. Secondly, these powers are universal. It is the reason why the Egyptians gave their gods animal appearances, and why totemic cultures (and today soccer or American football teams) recognize themselves in animal figures, be it the bull or the zebra, the donkey or the bear.

When the animal speaks and acts as a cartoon, it is the absolute that speaks, and that is why it is futile to wonder about the relationship between Donald Duck, Daisy Duck and Huey, Dewey, and Louie. Those are bourgeois details of little importance, what goes on stage are the great themes: Nemo in search of his father like Telemachus in the Odyssey; the dog Lady who tries to understand what true love is; what the right form of government is according to the experience of the lion king Simba; what it means to be different for an elephant like Dumbo; if the sublime can be depicted by Ponyo walking on stormy waves. These are the great themes, the same ones that were dealt with in nineteenth-century novels, and which have been abandoned in favour of self-referential tales and facts, or of works of visual art that require an explanation not to be confused with neon tubes.

MIMESIS GROUP
www.mimesis-group.com

MIMESIS INTERNATIONAL
www.mimesisinternational.com
info@mimesisinternational.com

MIMESIS EDIZIONI
www.mimesisedizioni.it
mimesis@mimesisedizioni.it

ÉDITIONS MIMÉSIS
www.editionsmimesis.fr
info@editionsmimesis.fr

MIMESIS COMMUNICATION
www.mim-c.net

MIMESIS EU
www.mim-eu.com

Printed by
Geca Industrie Grafiche – San Giuliano Milanese (MI)
August 2019